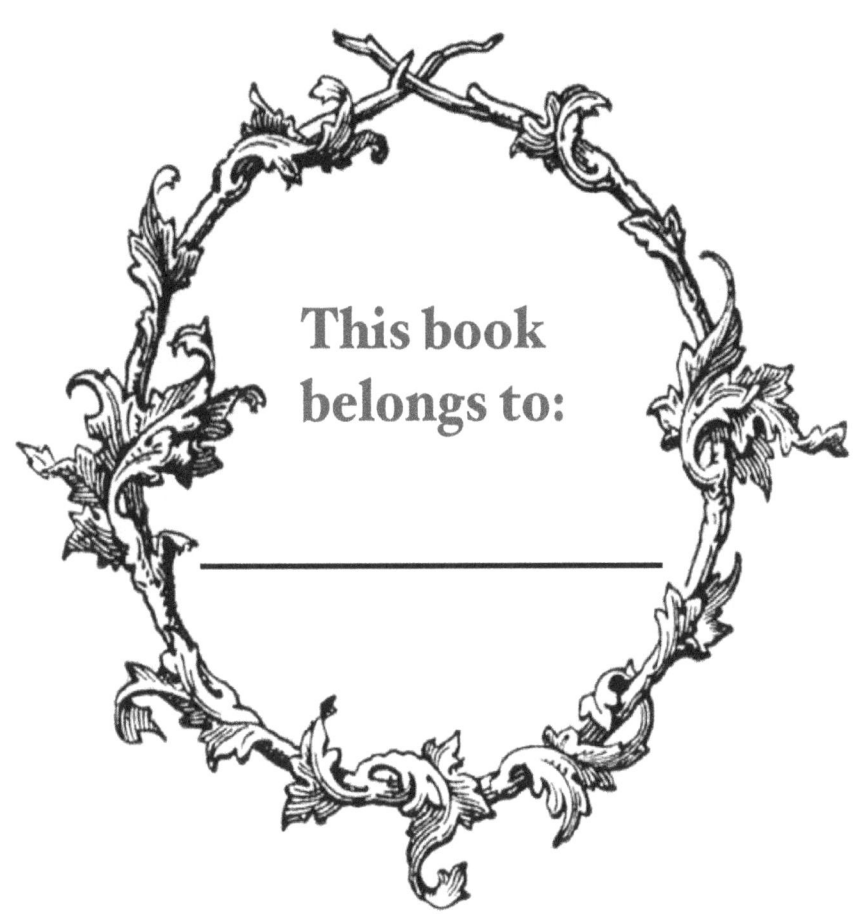

This book
belongs to:

_____

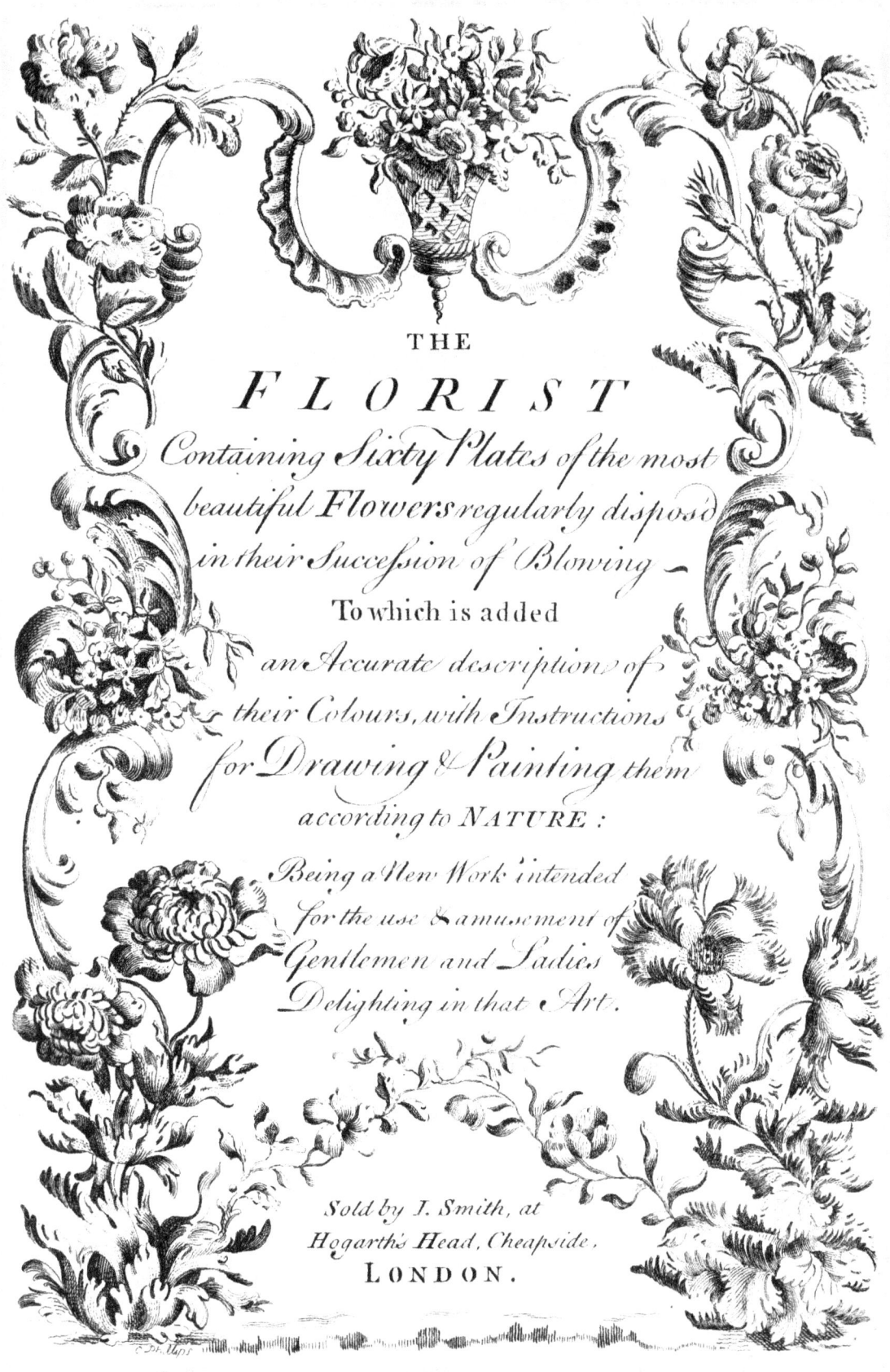

THE

FLORIST

Containing Sixty Plates of the most

beautiful Flowers regularly dispos'd

in their Succession of Blowing —

To which is added

an Accurate description of

their Colours, with Instructions

for Drawing & Painting them

according to NATURE :

Being a New Work intended

for the use & amusement of

Gentlemen and Ladies

Delighting in that Art.

Sold by J. Smith, at

Hogarth's Head, Cheapside,

LONDON.

Pl. *1*

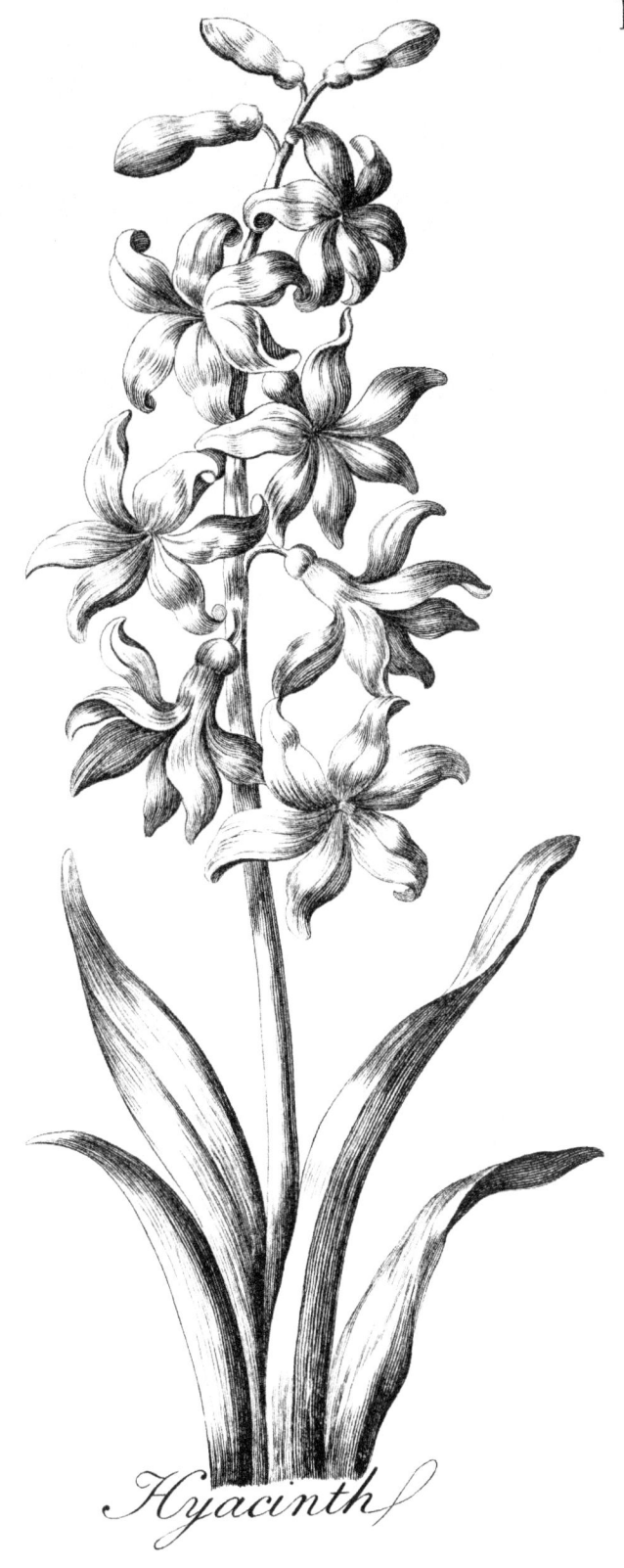

Hyacinth

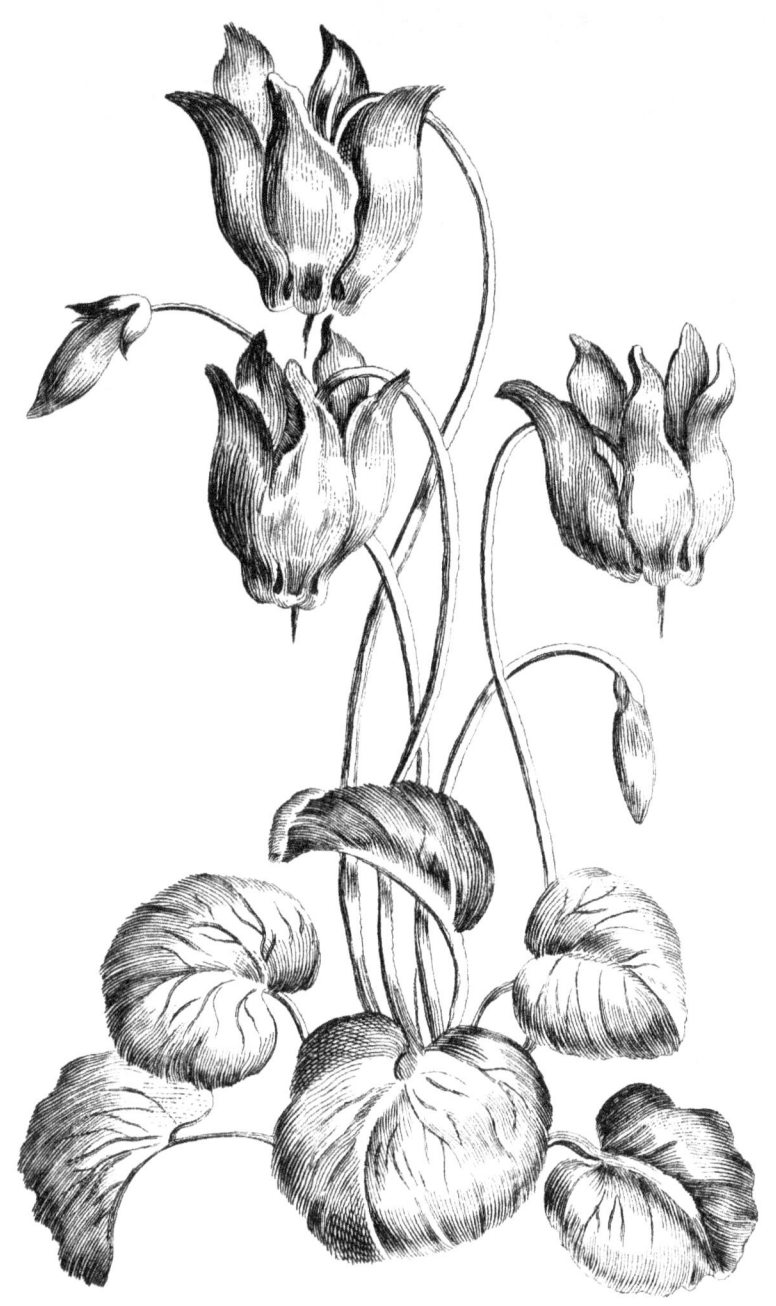

Cydamen

Pl. 3

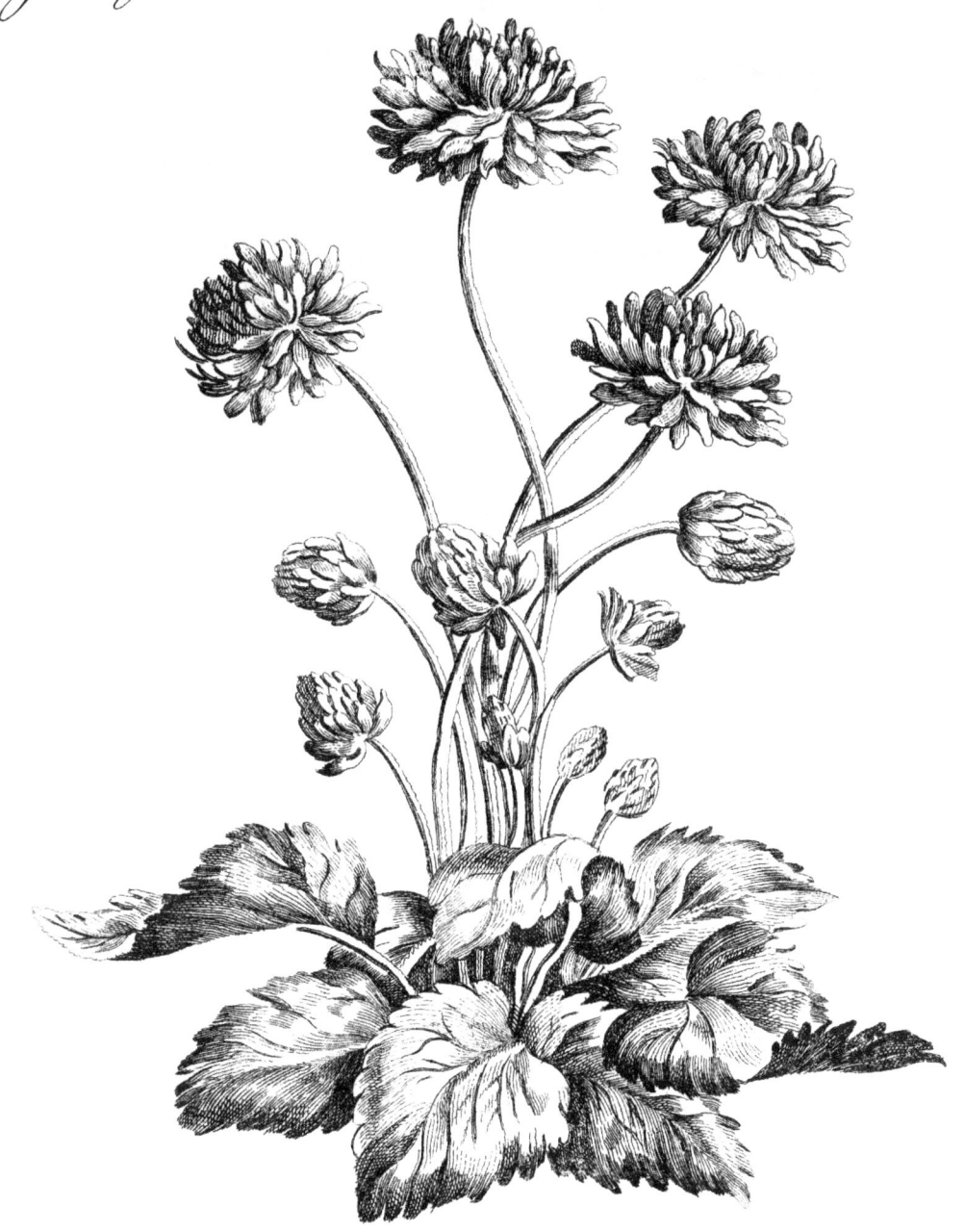

Crowfoot

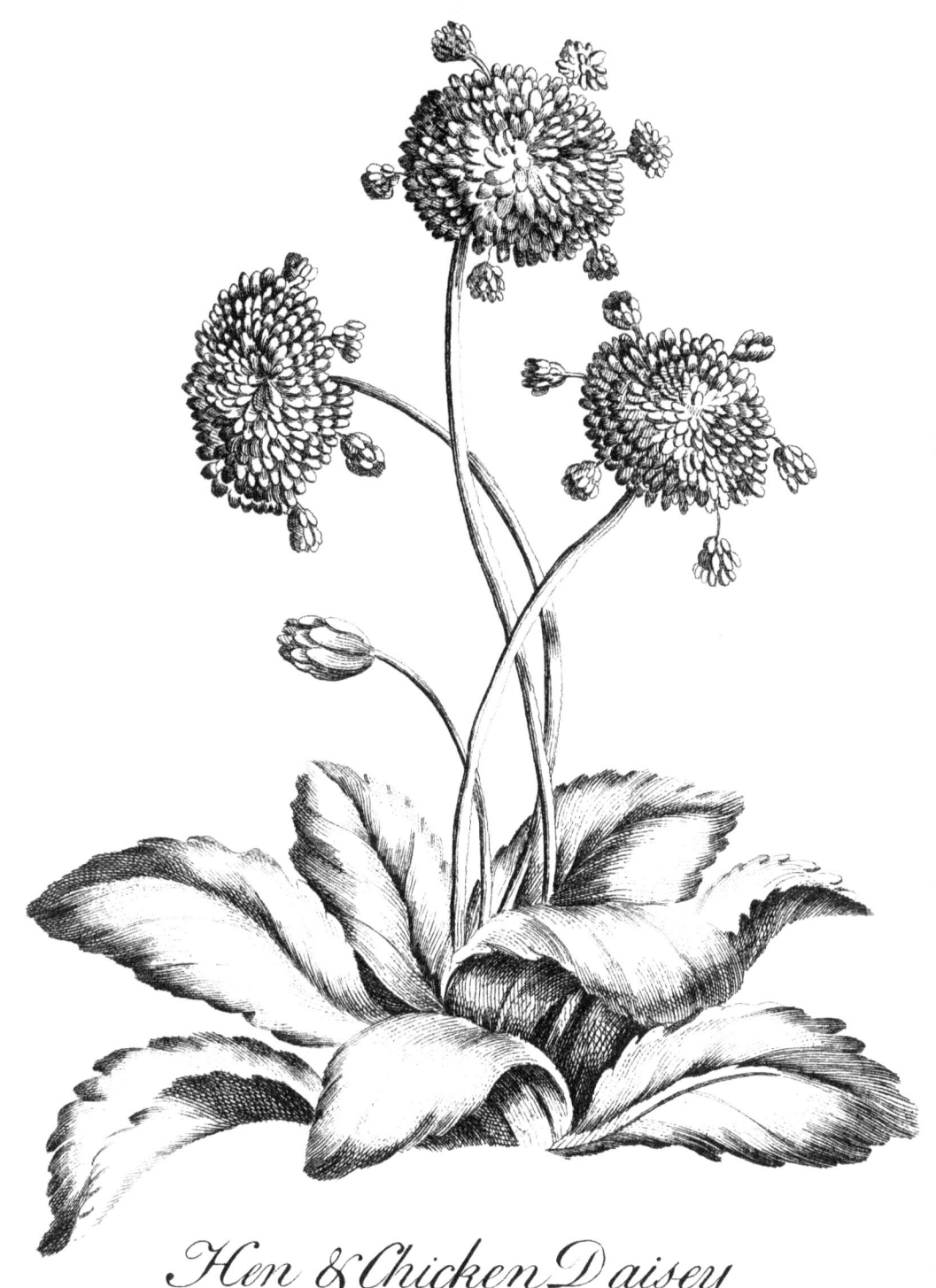

Hen & Chicken Daisey

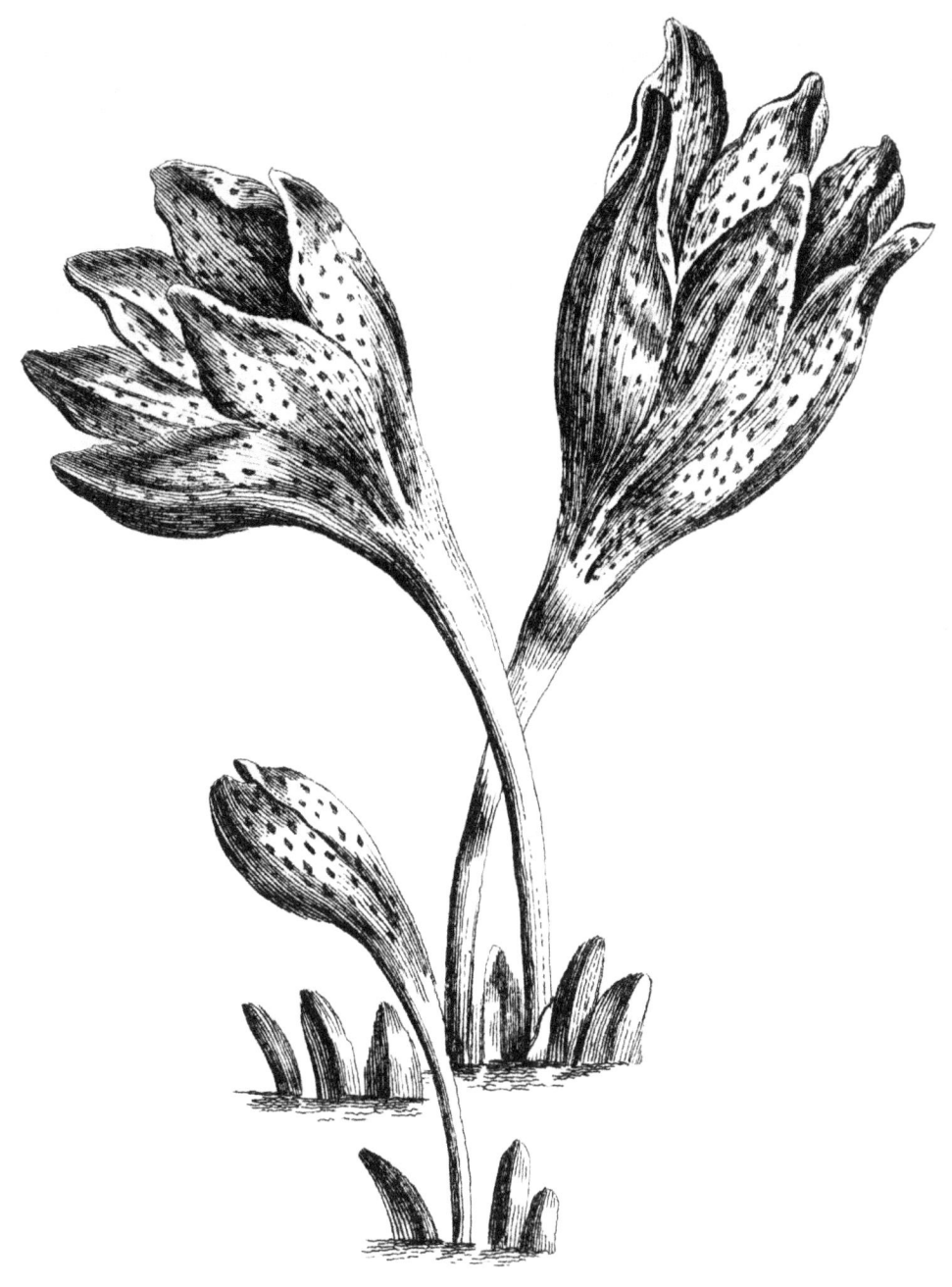

Colchicum

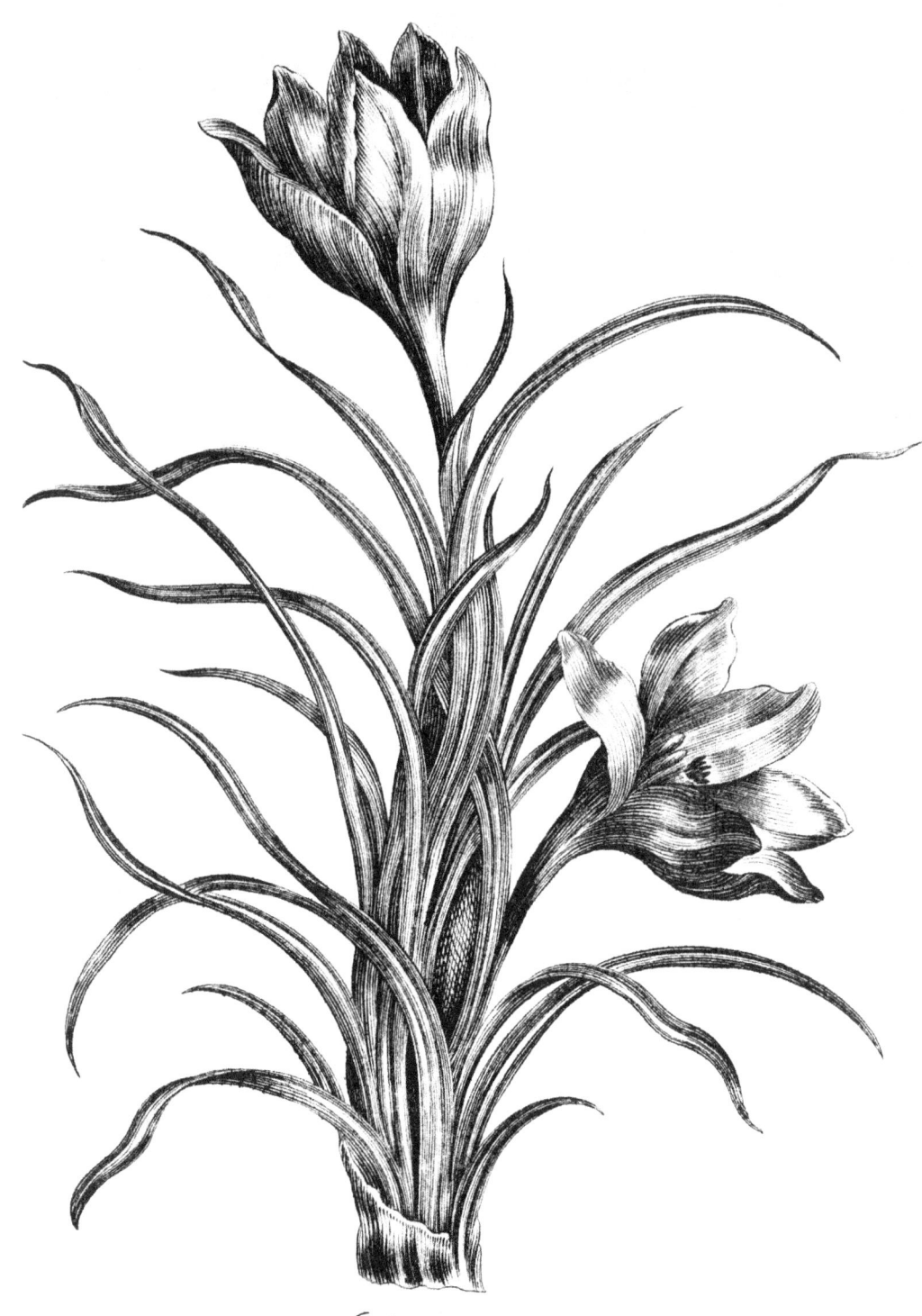

Crocus

Pl. 7

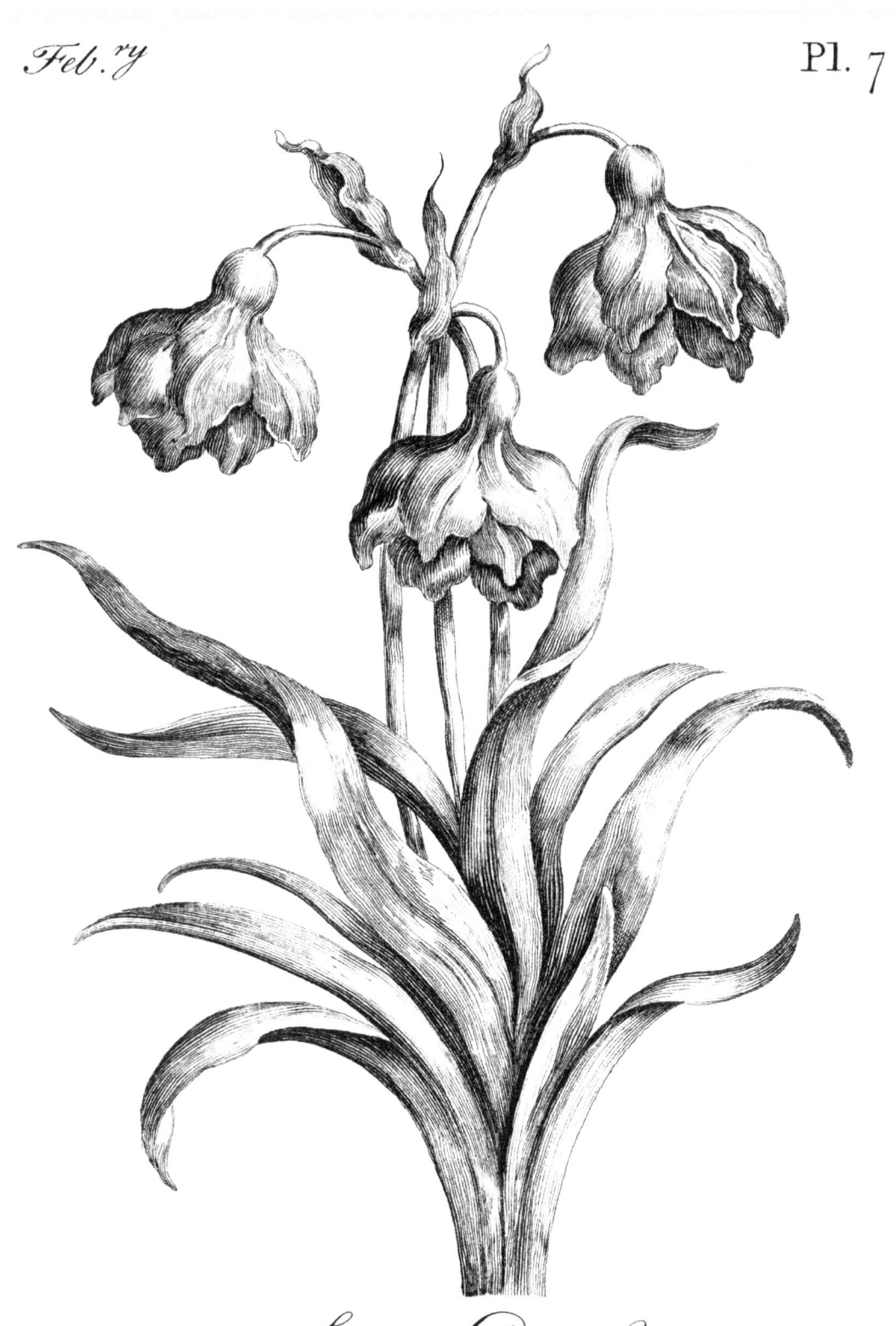

Snow Drop

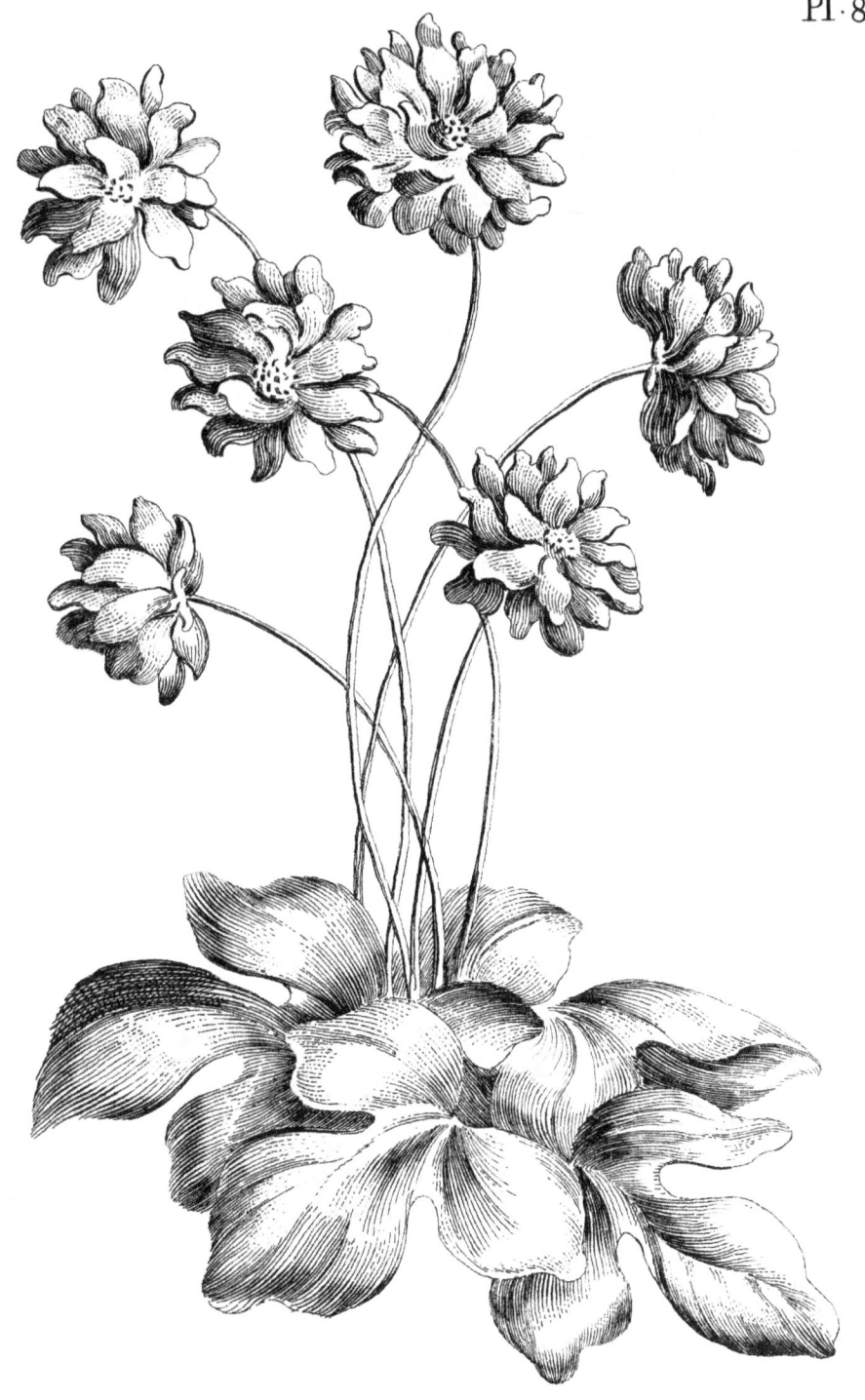

Double Hepatica.

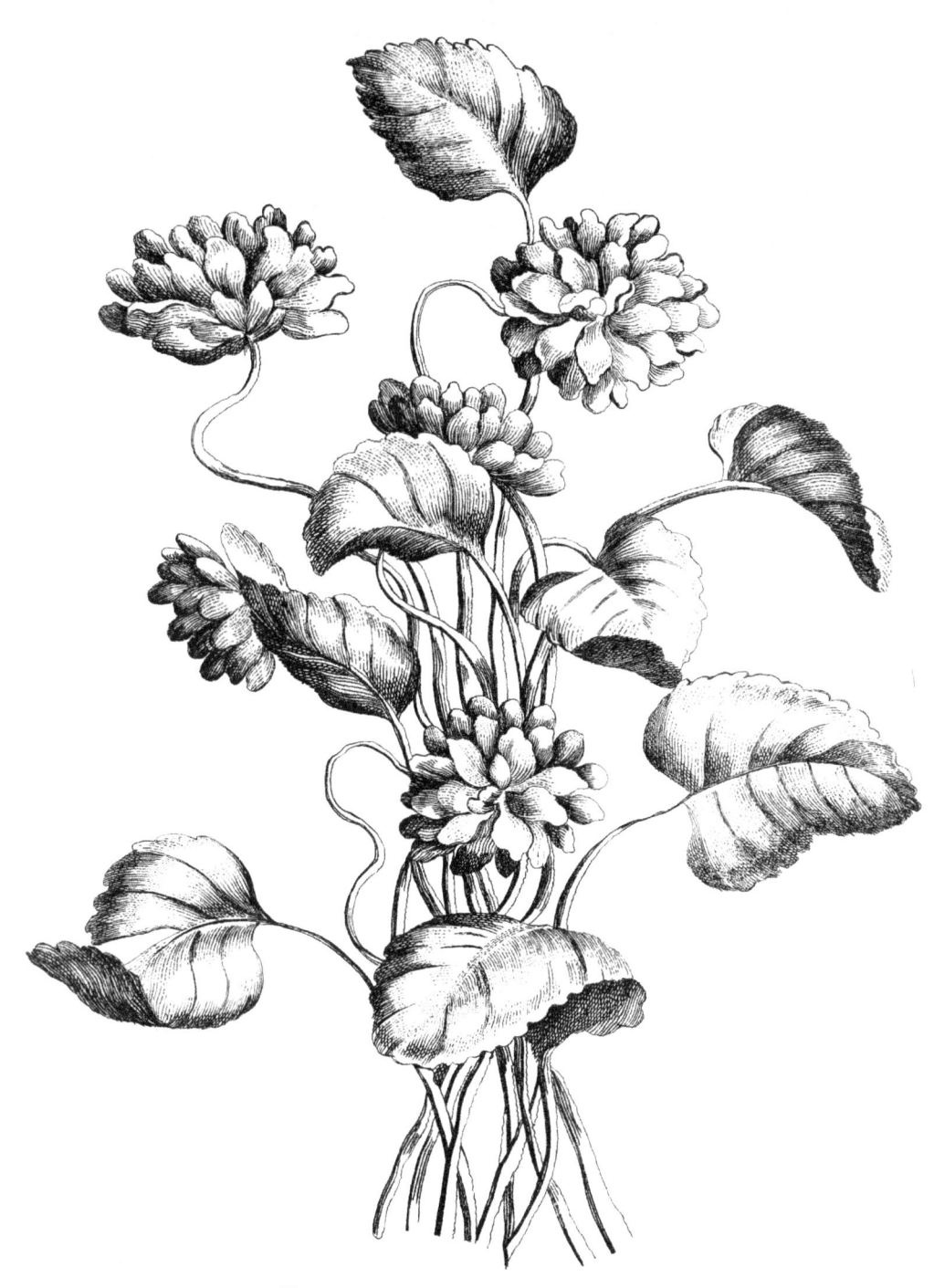

Double Violet

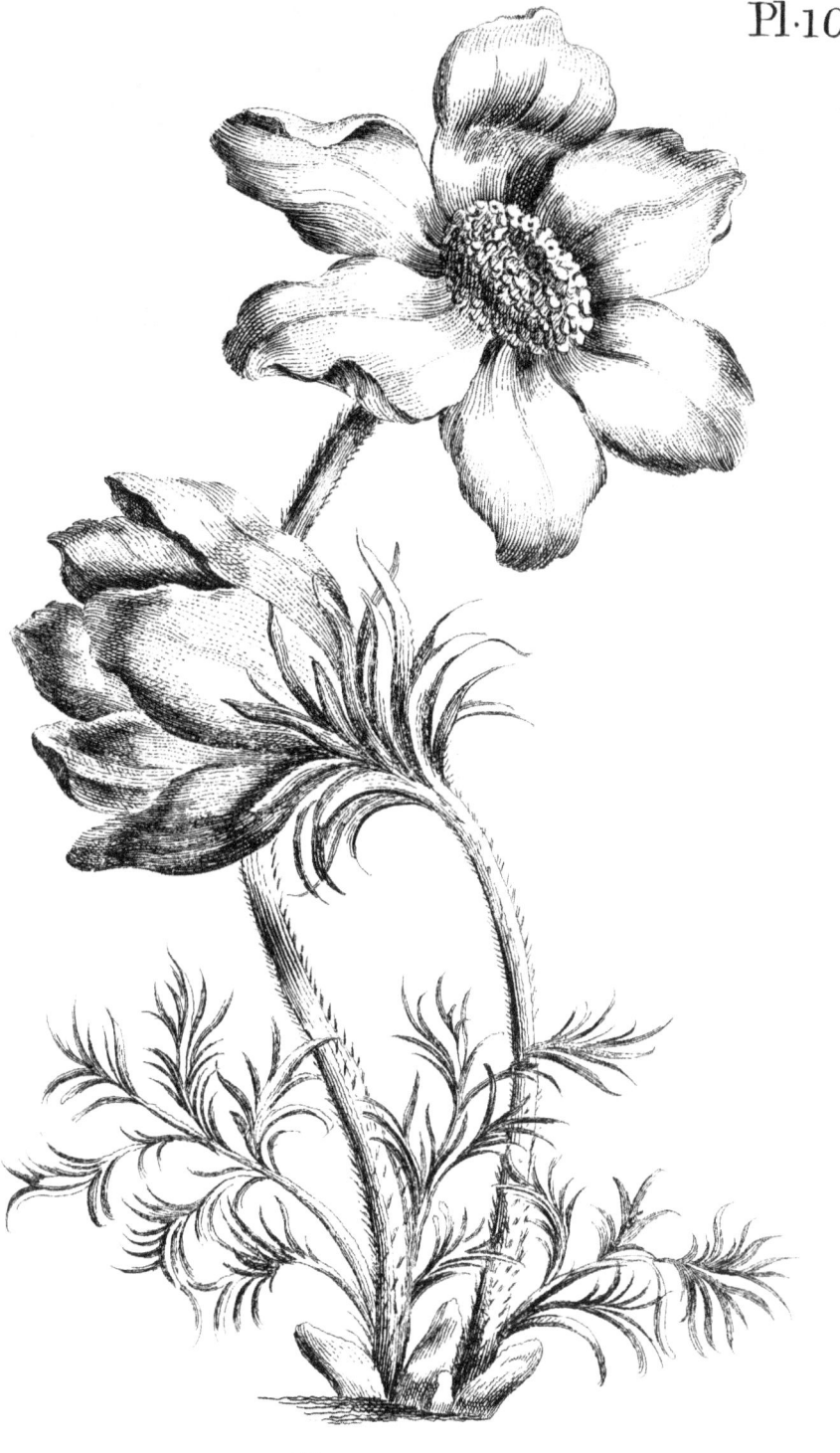

Pasque Flower

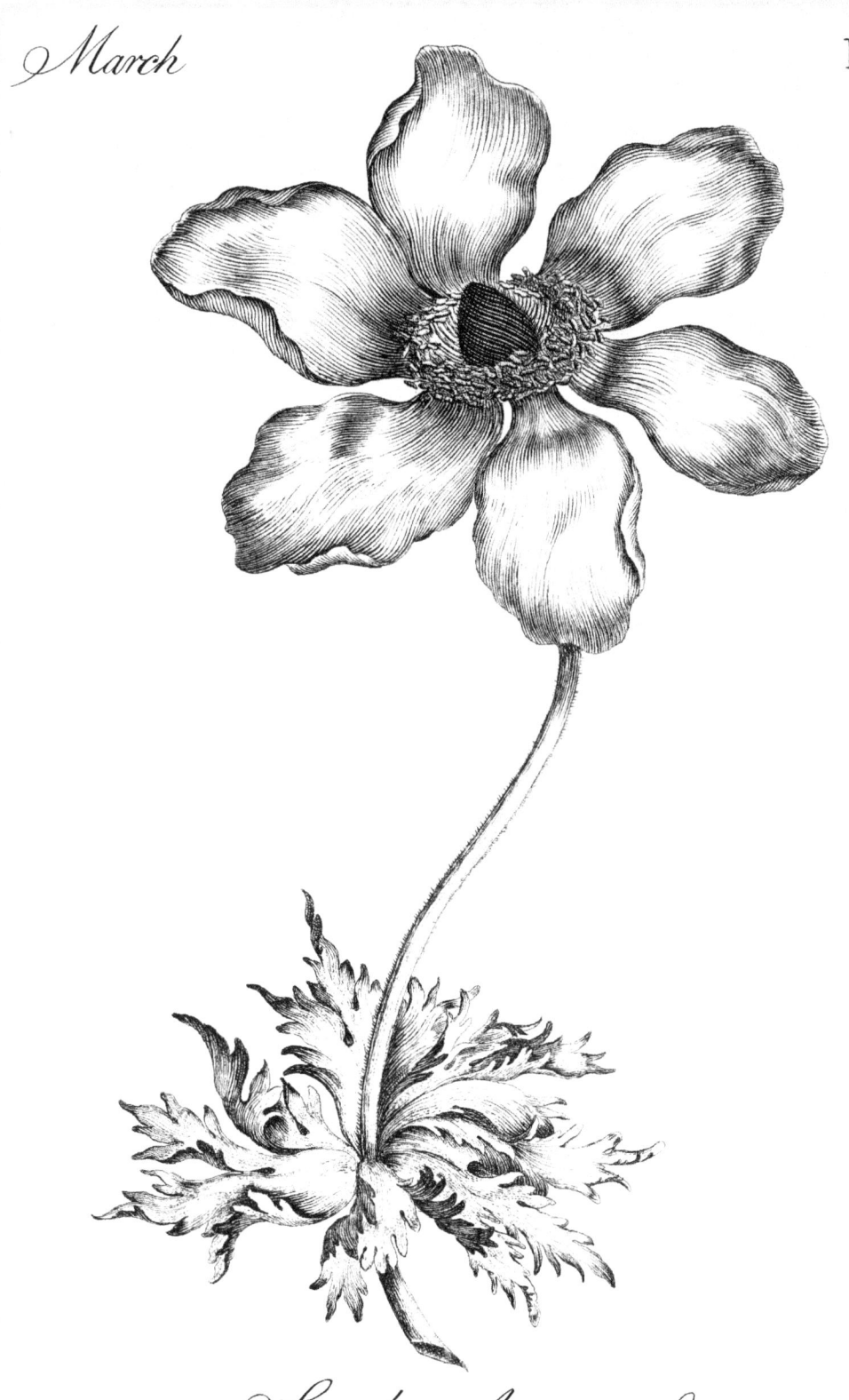

Single Anemone

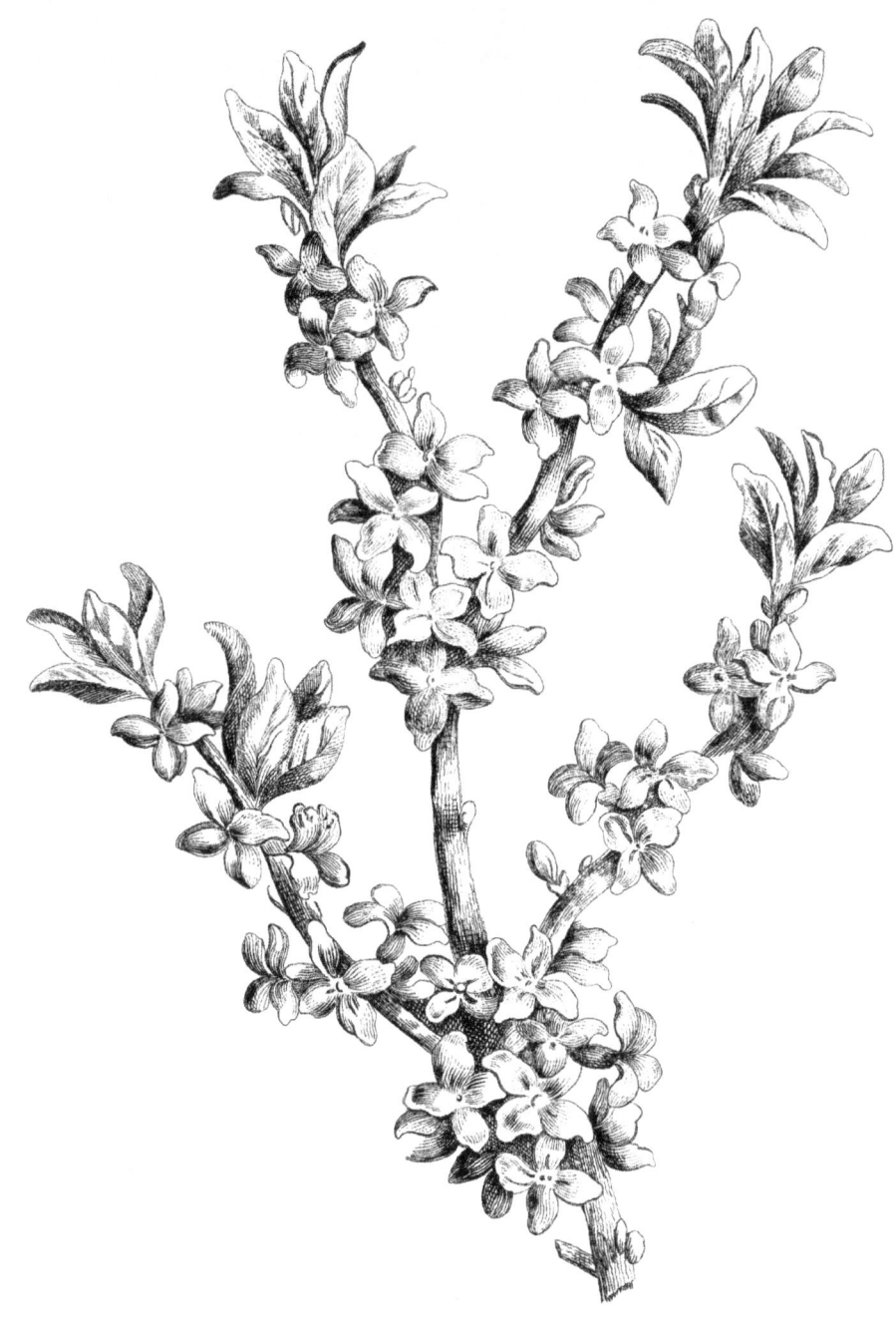

Mezereon

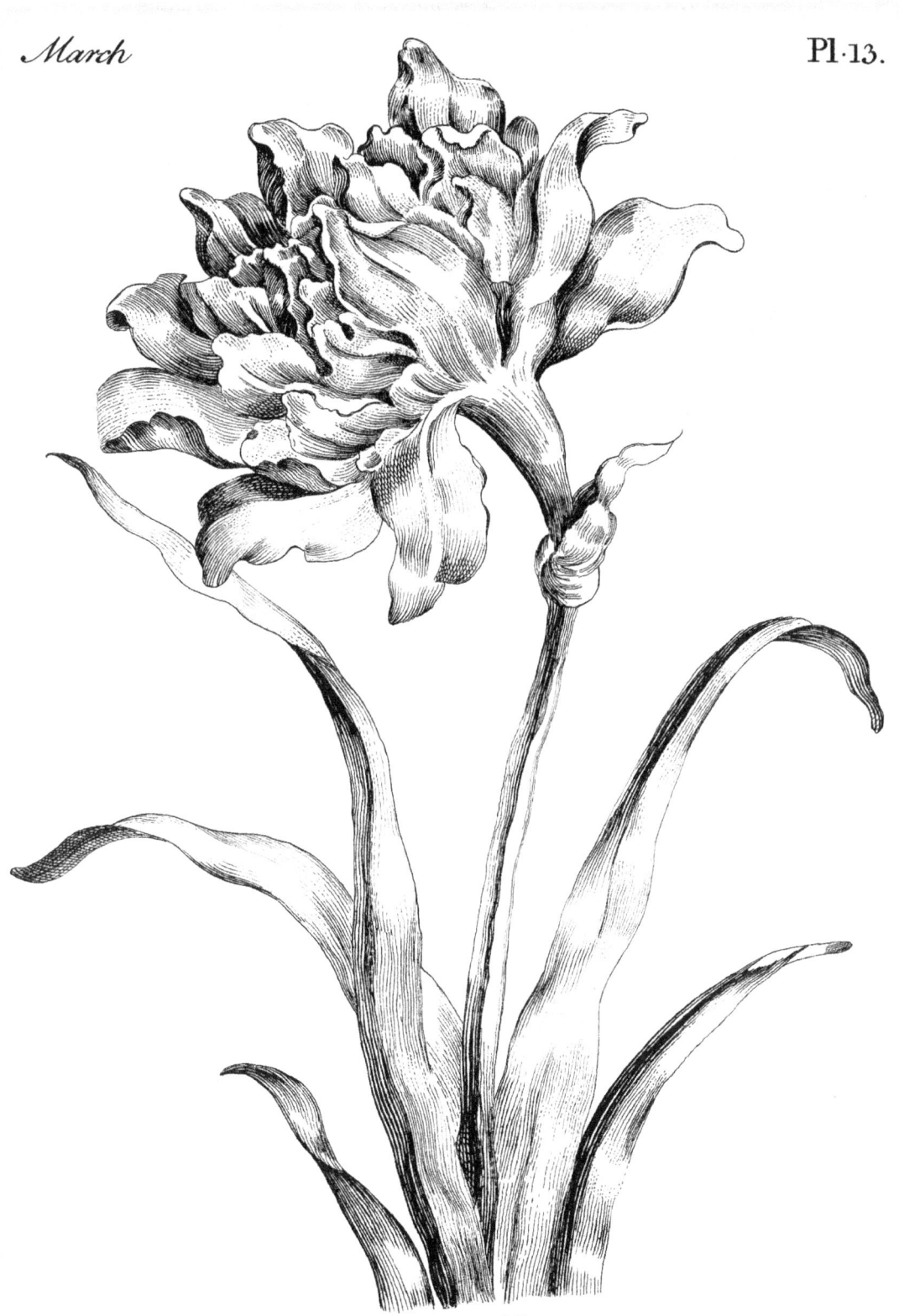

Double Daffodill

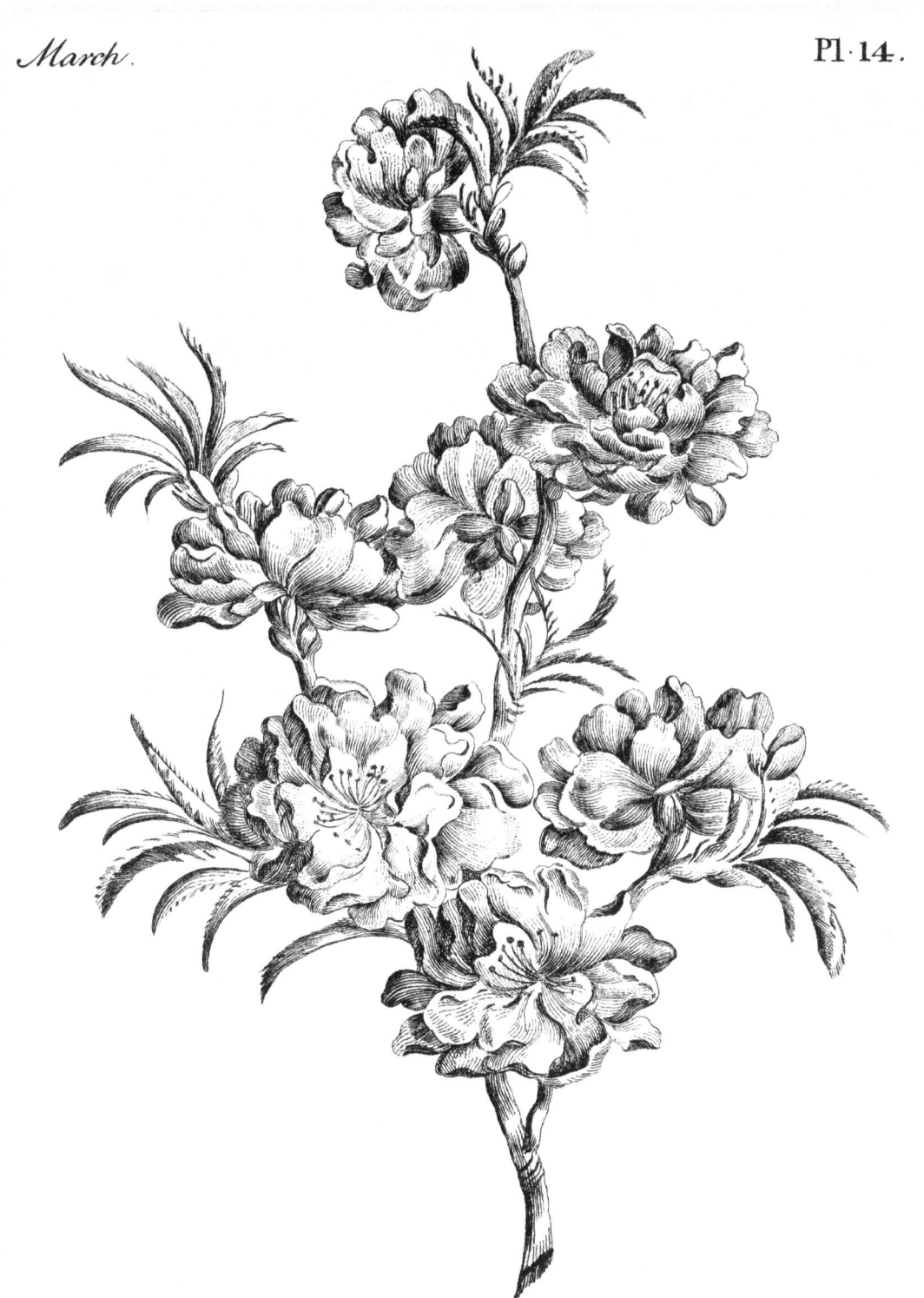

Double Almond Blossom

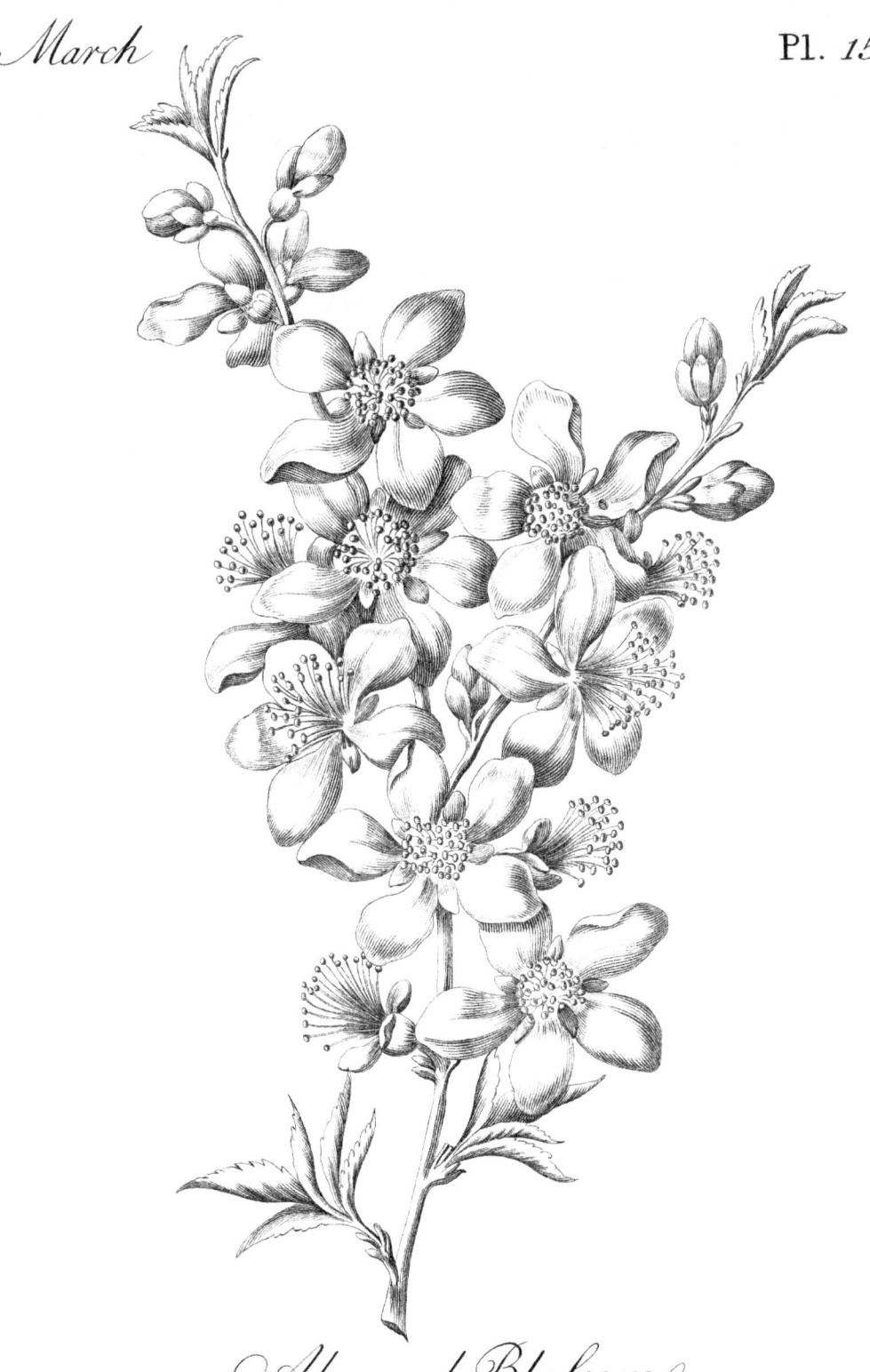

Almond Blossom

Pl. *16*

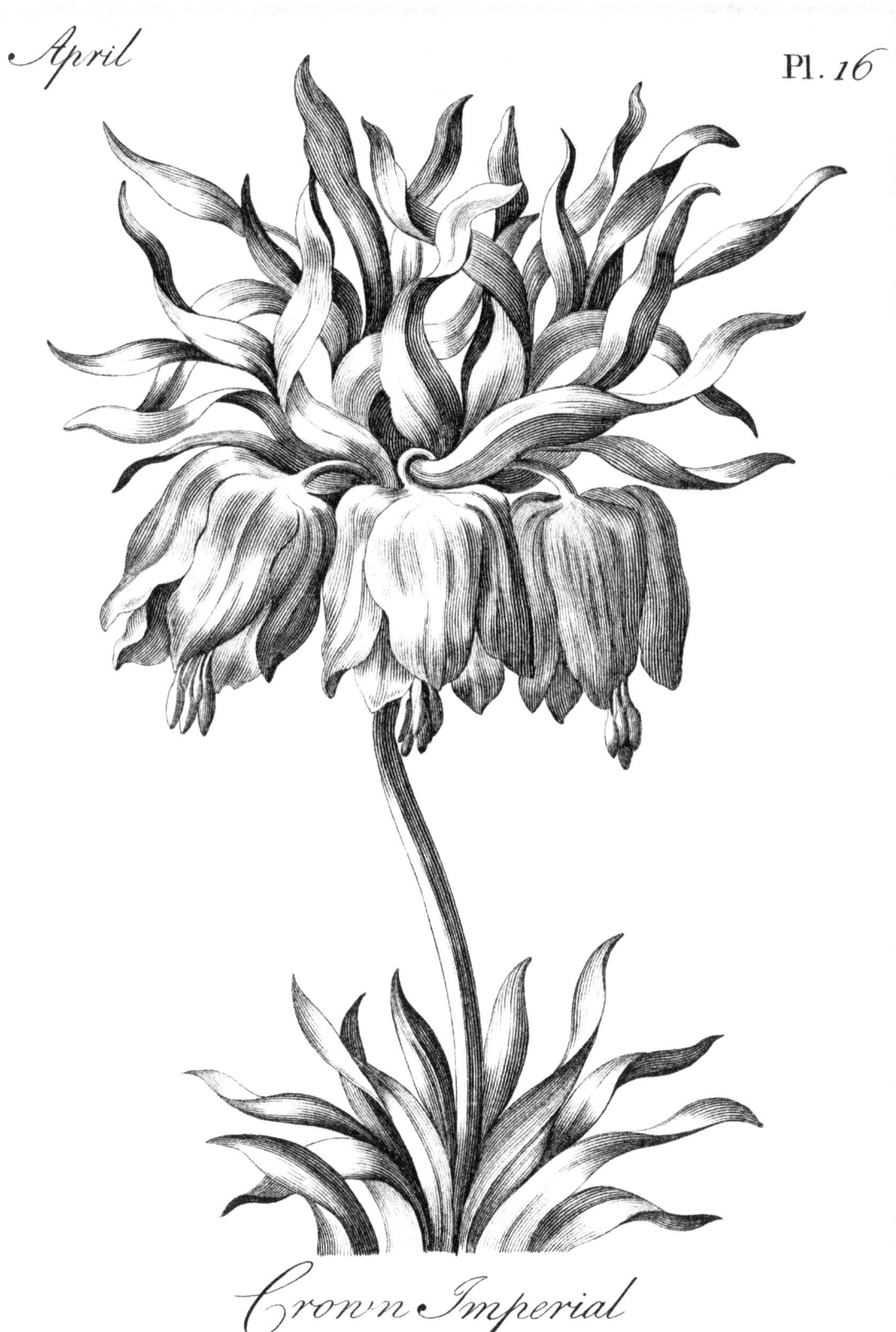

Crown Imperial

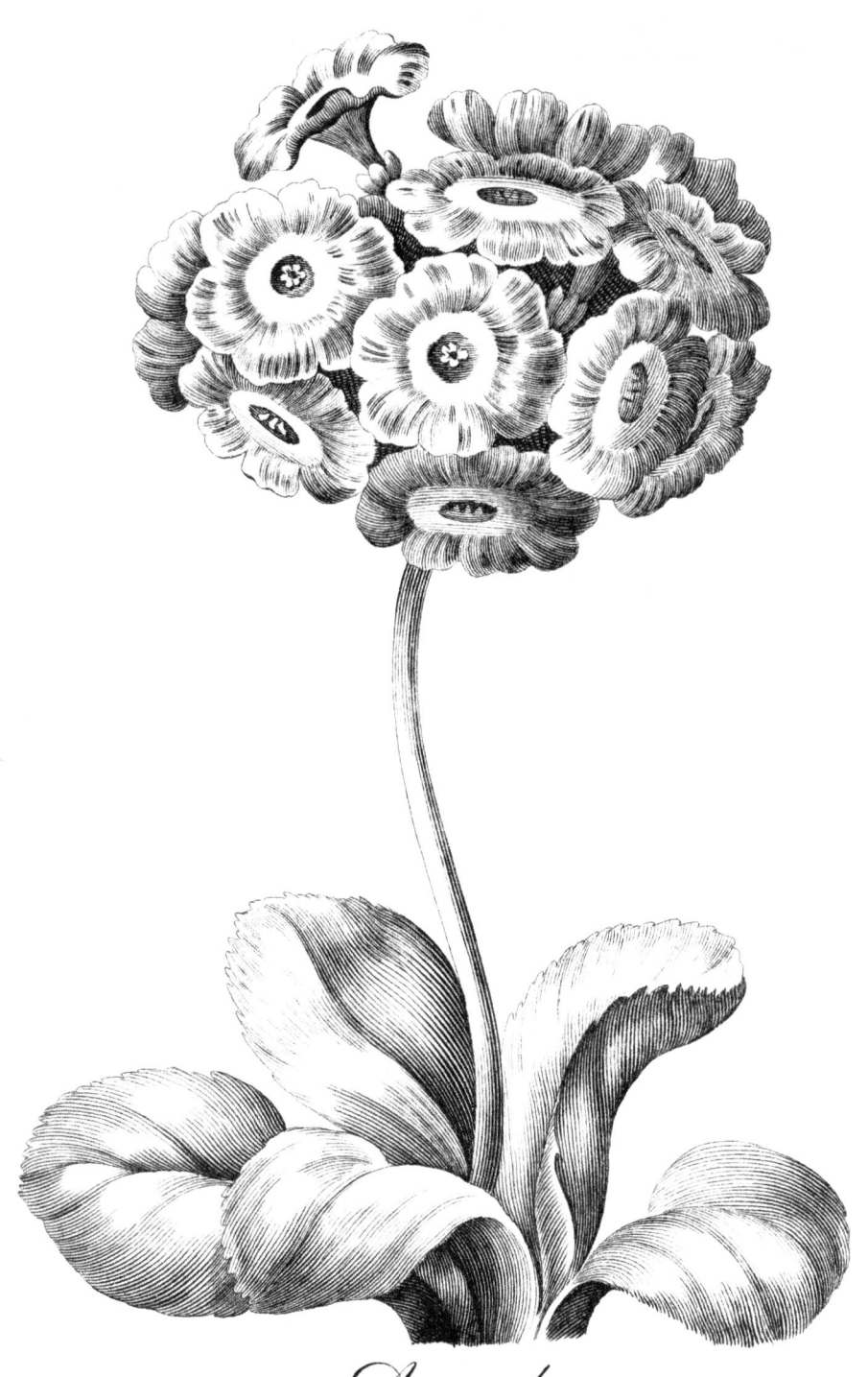

Auricula

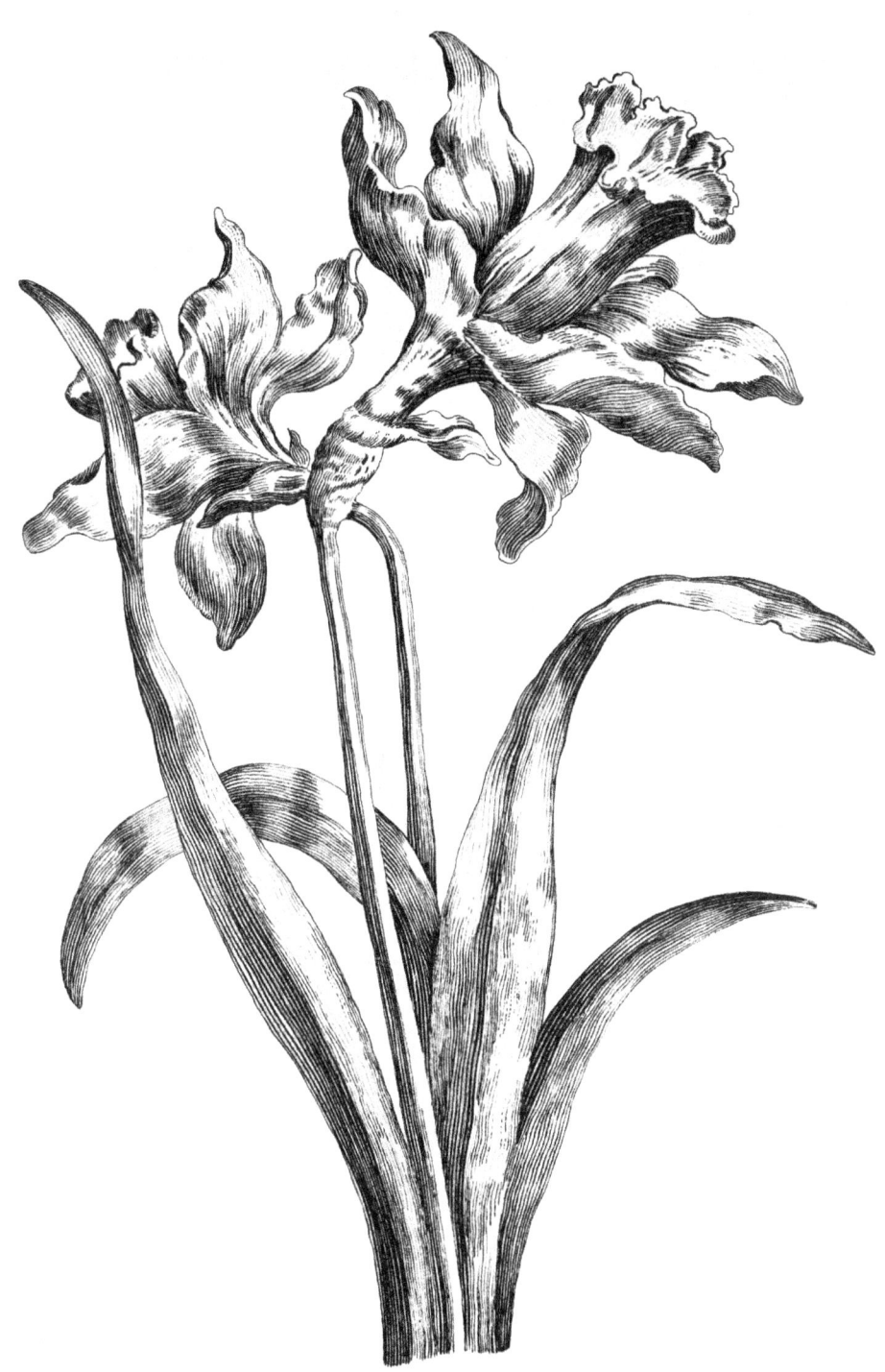

Daffodil.

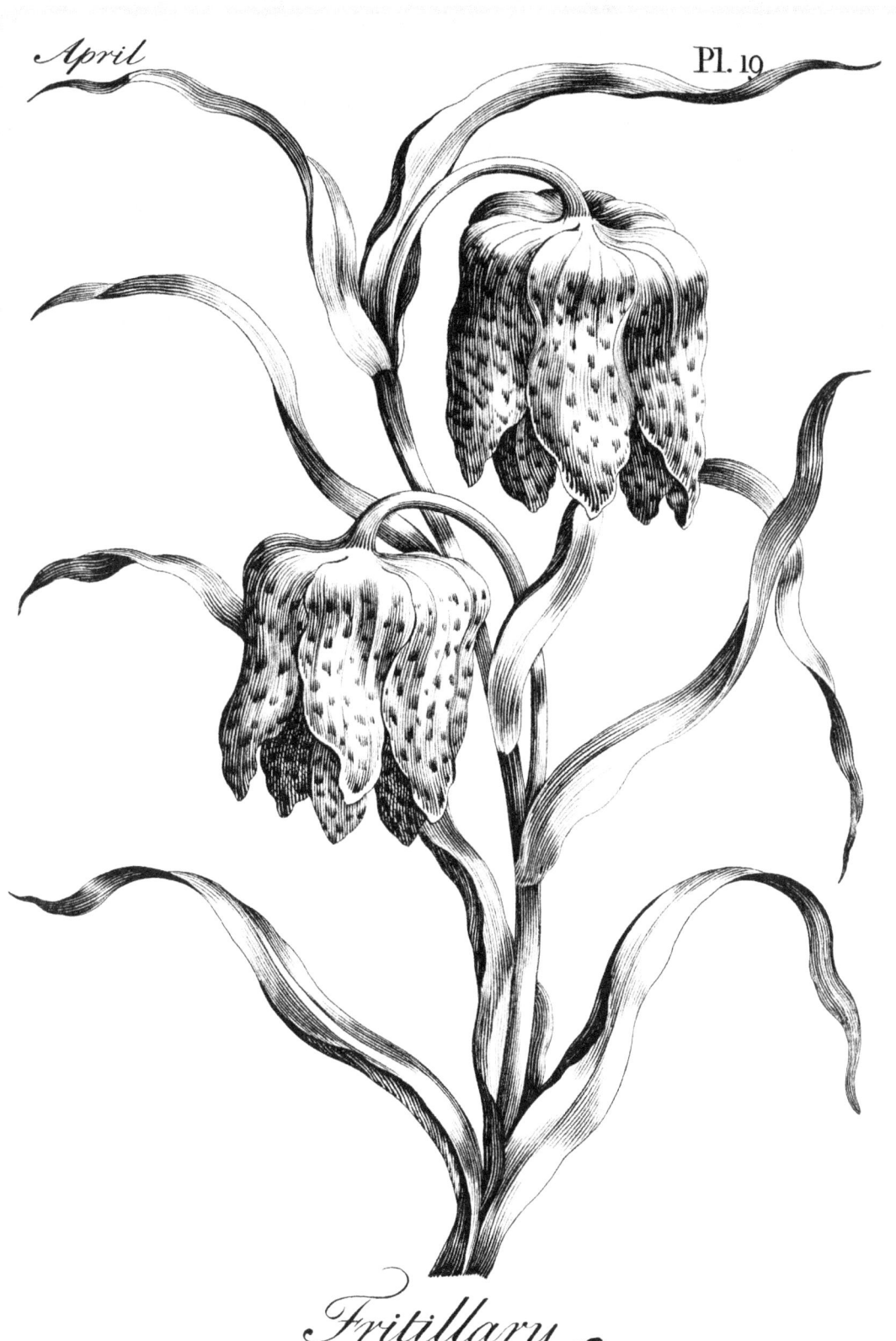

Fritillary.

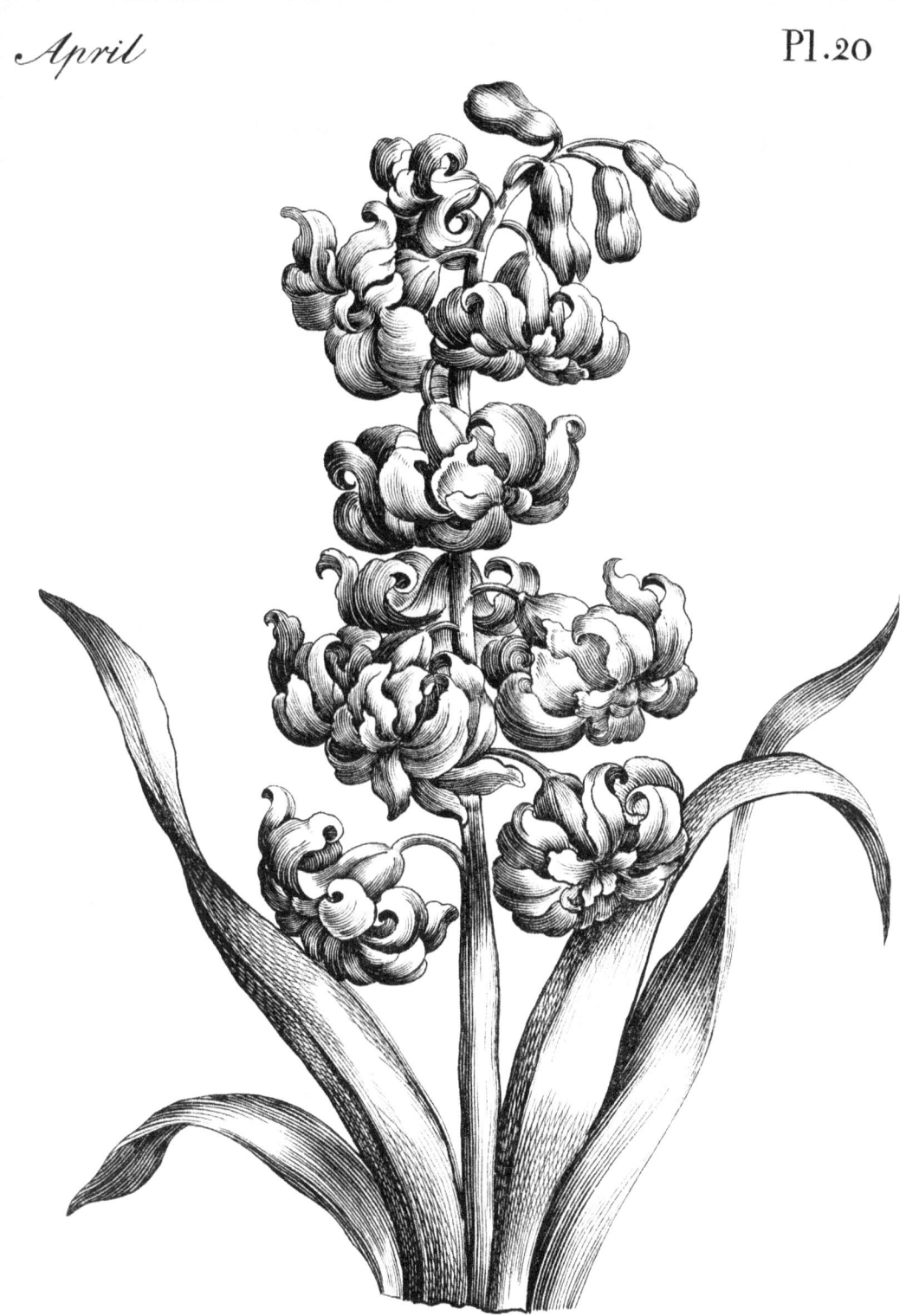

Double Hyacinth

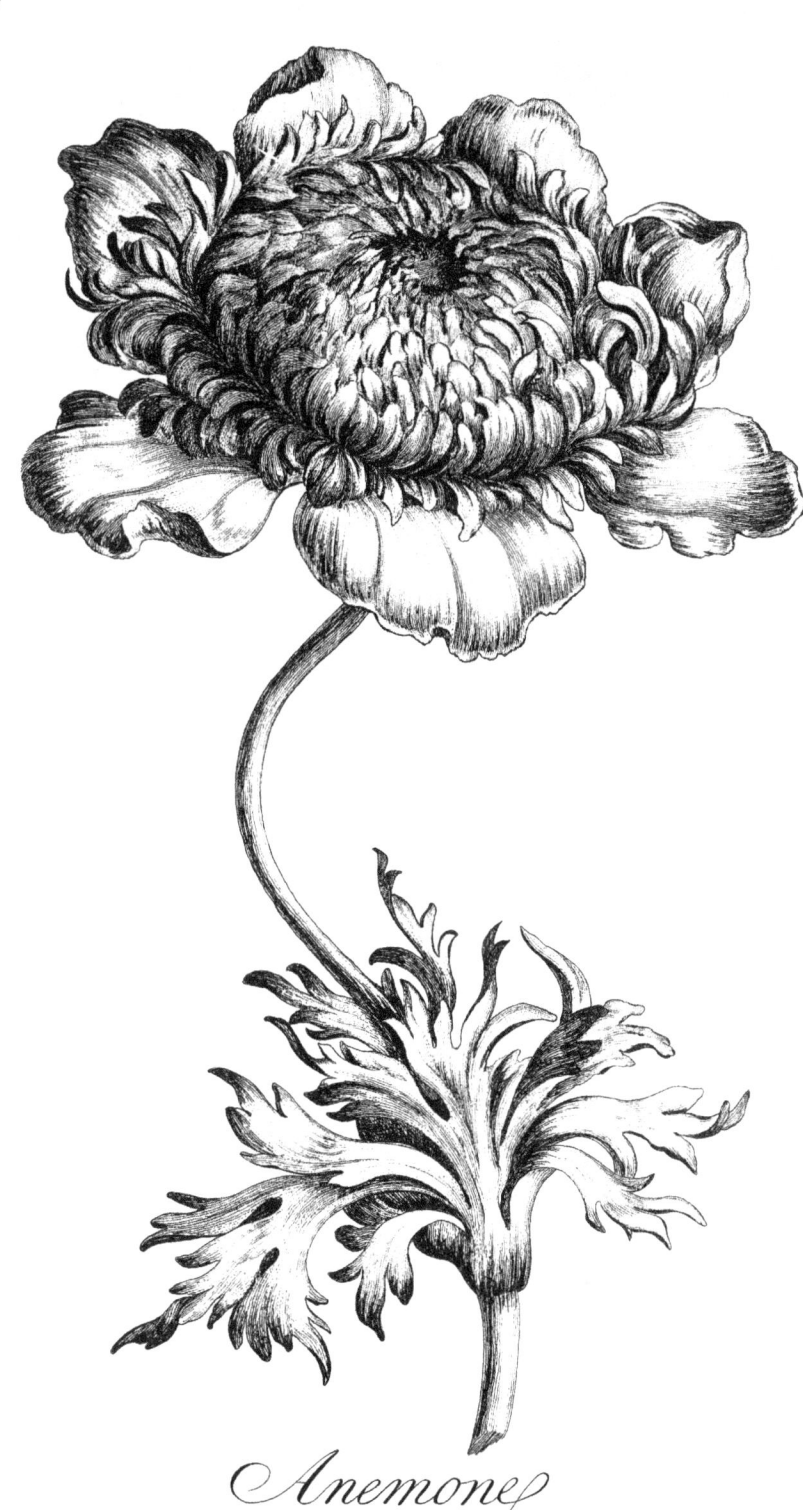

Anemone

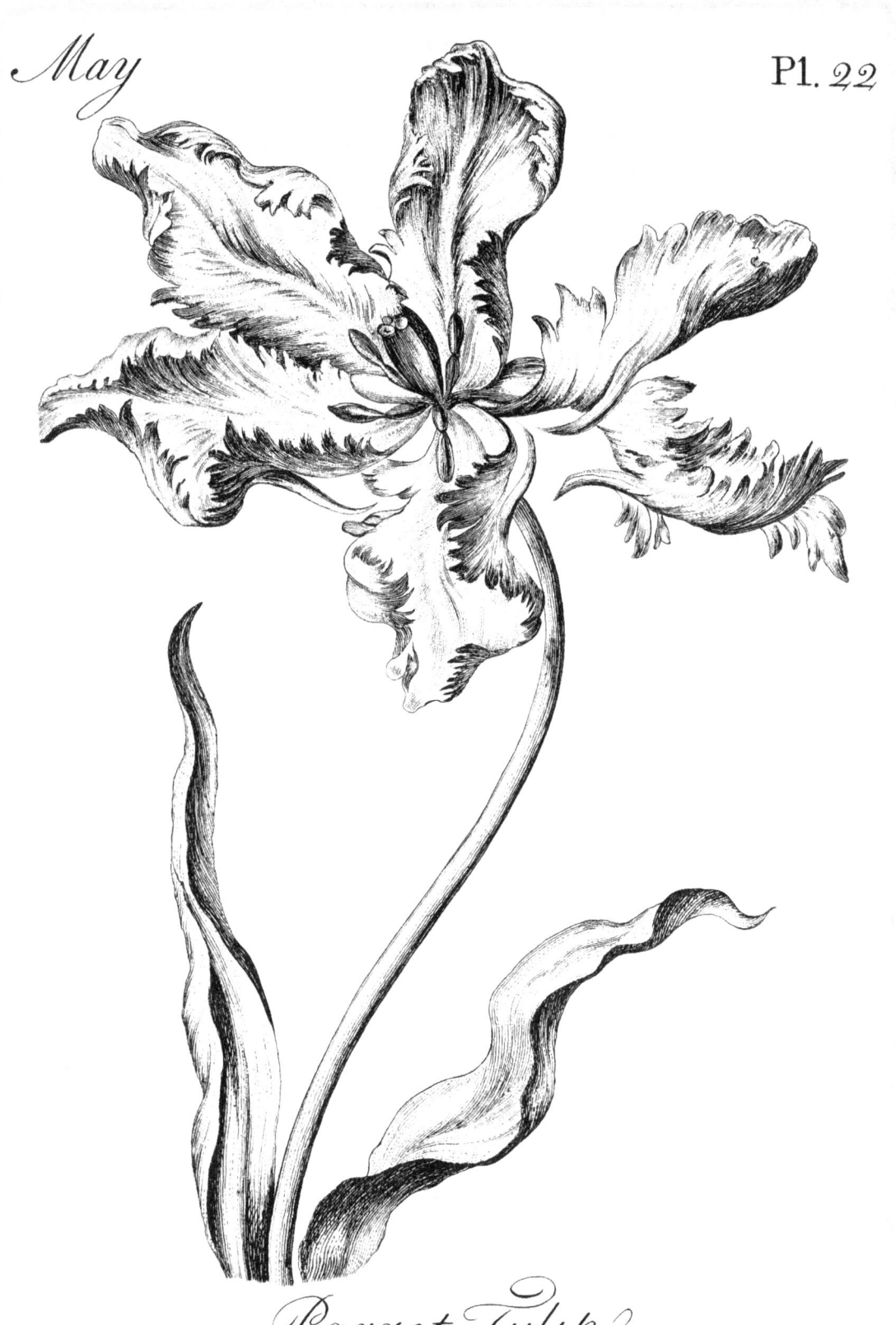

Parrot Tulip

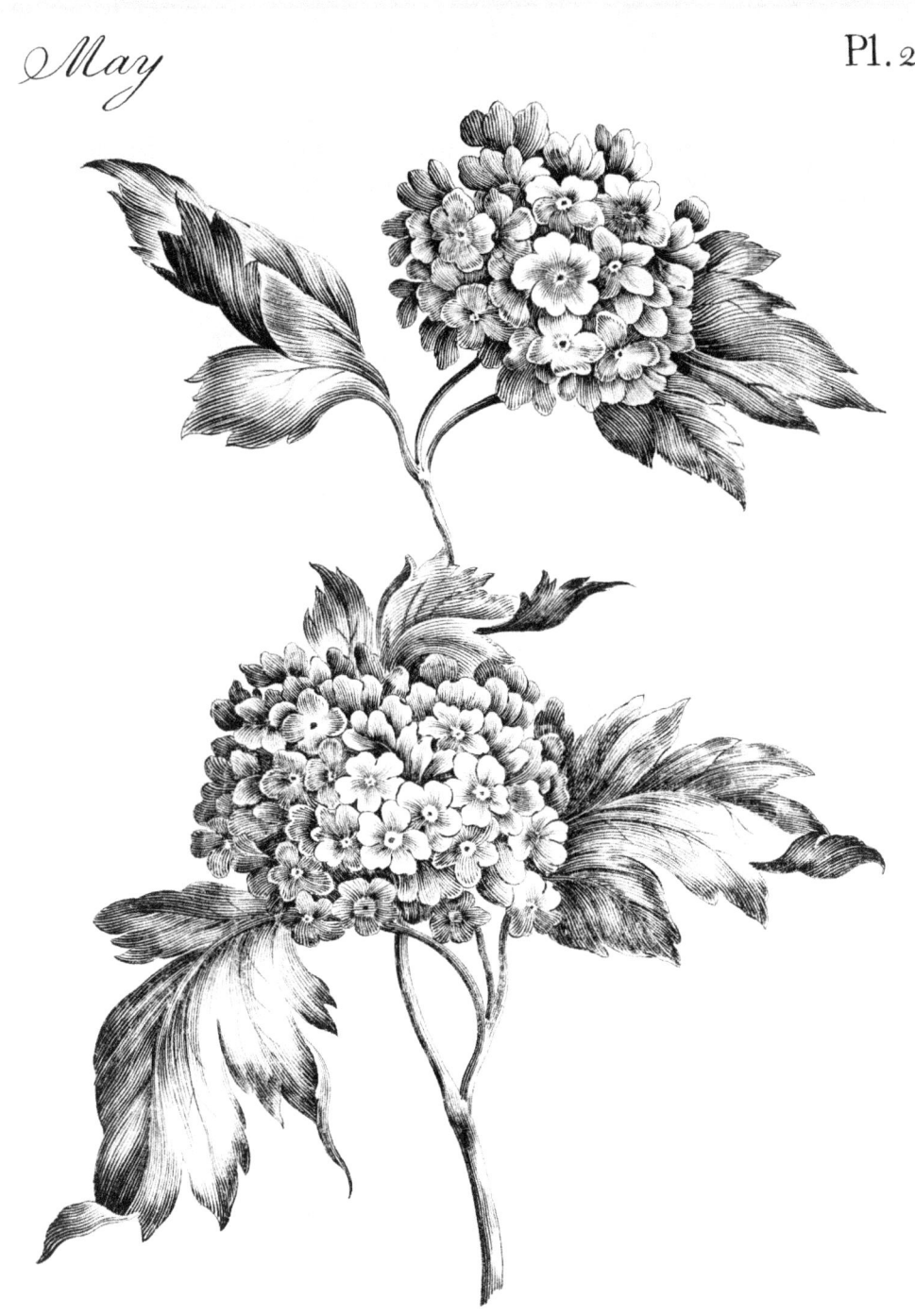

Guelder Rose

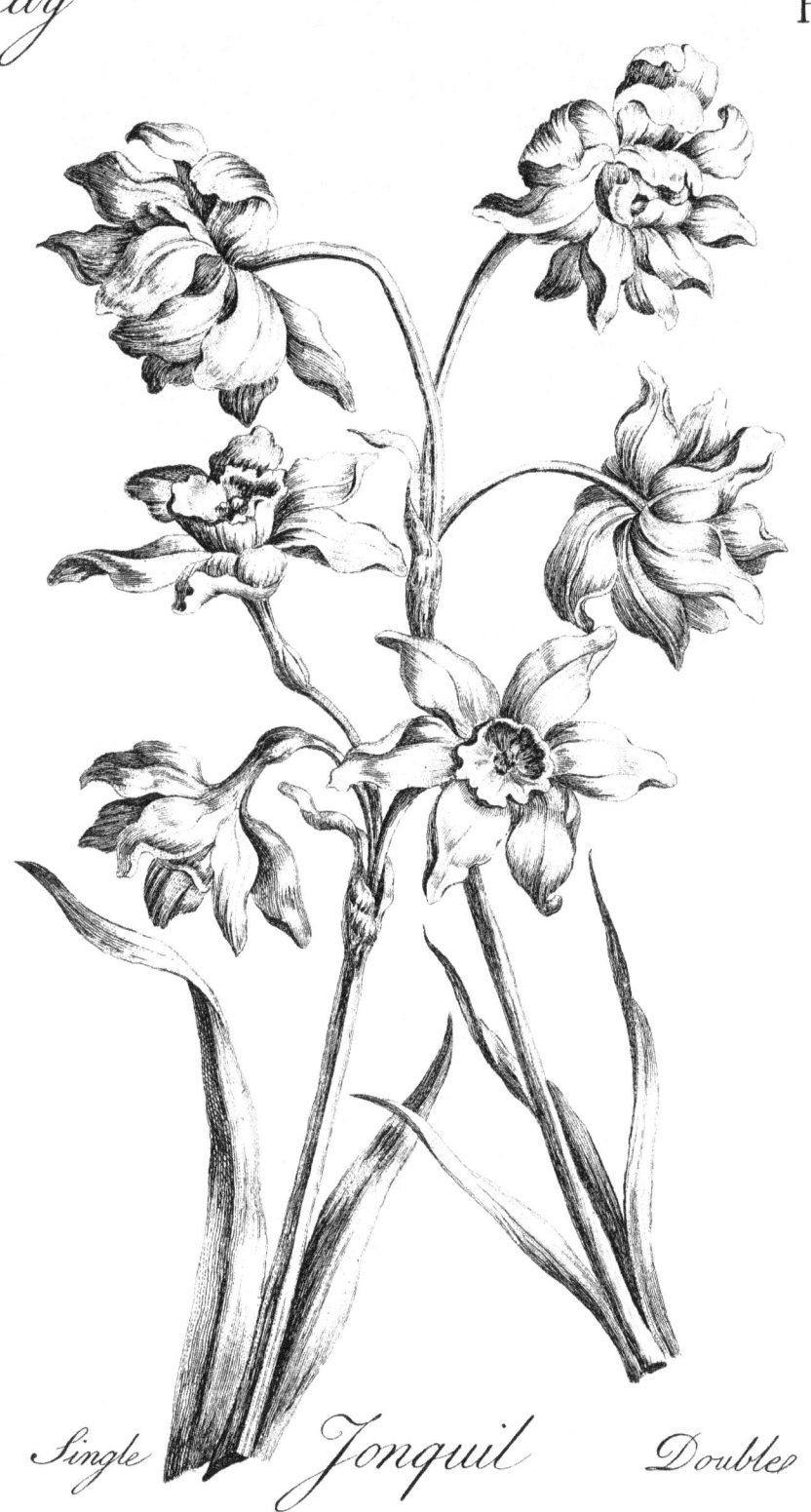

Single Jonquil *Double*

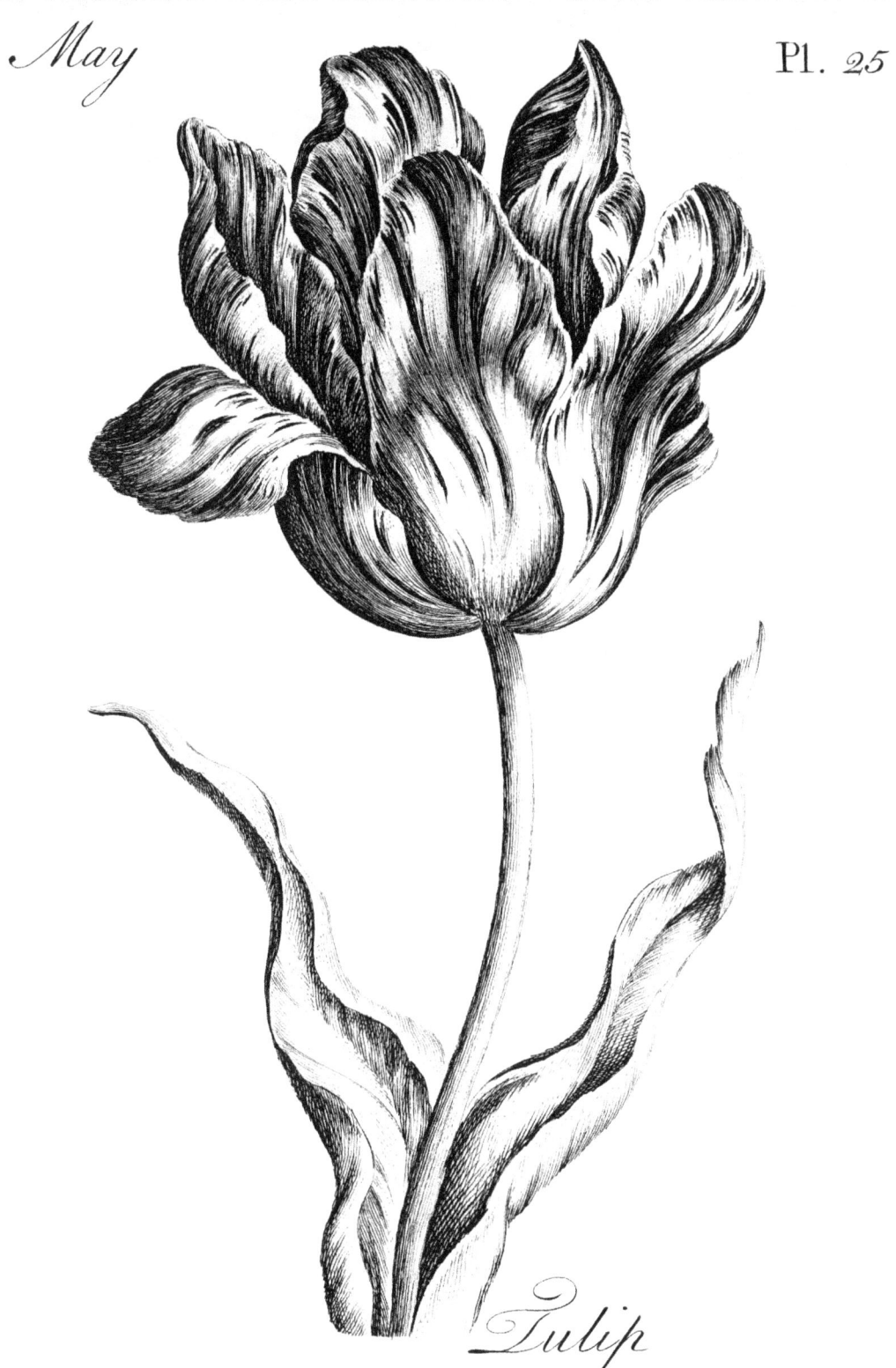

Tulip

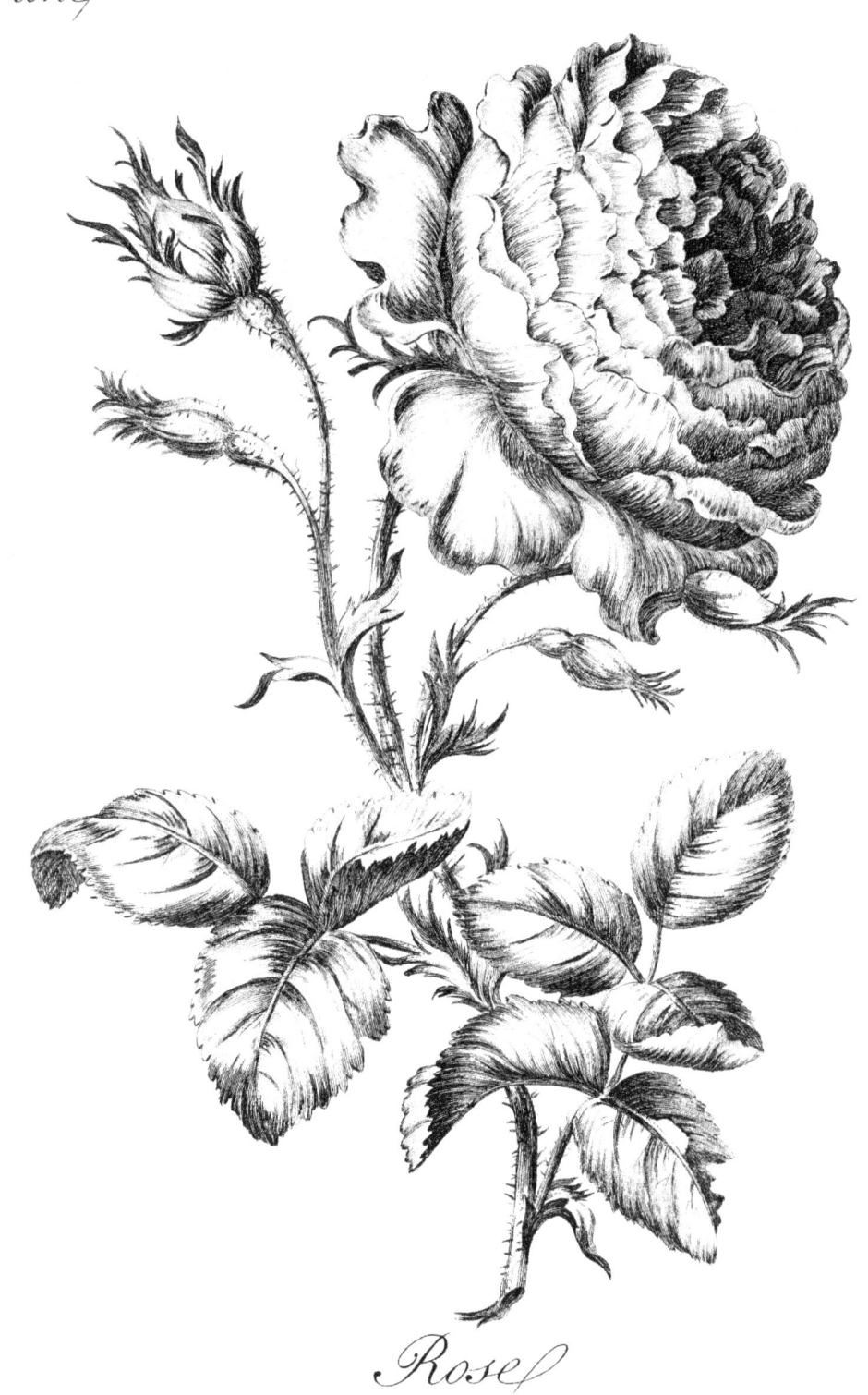

Rose

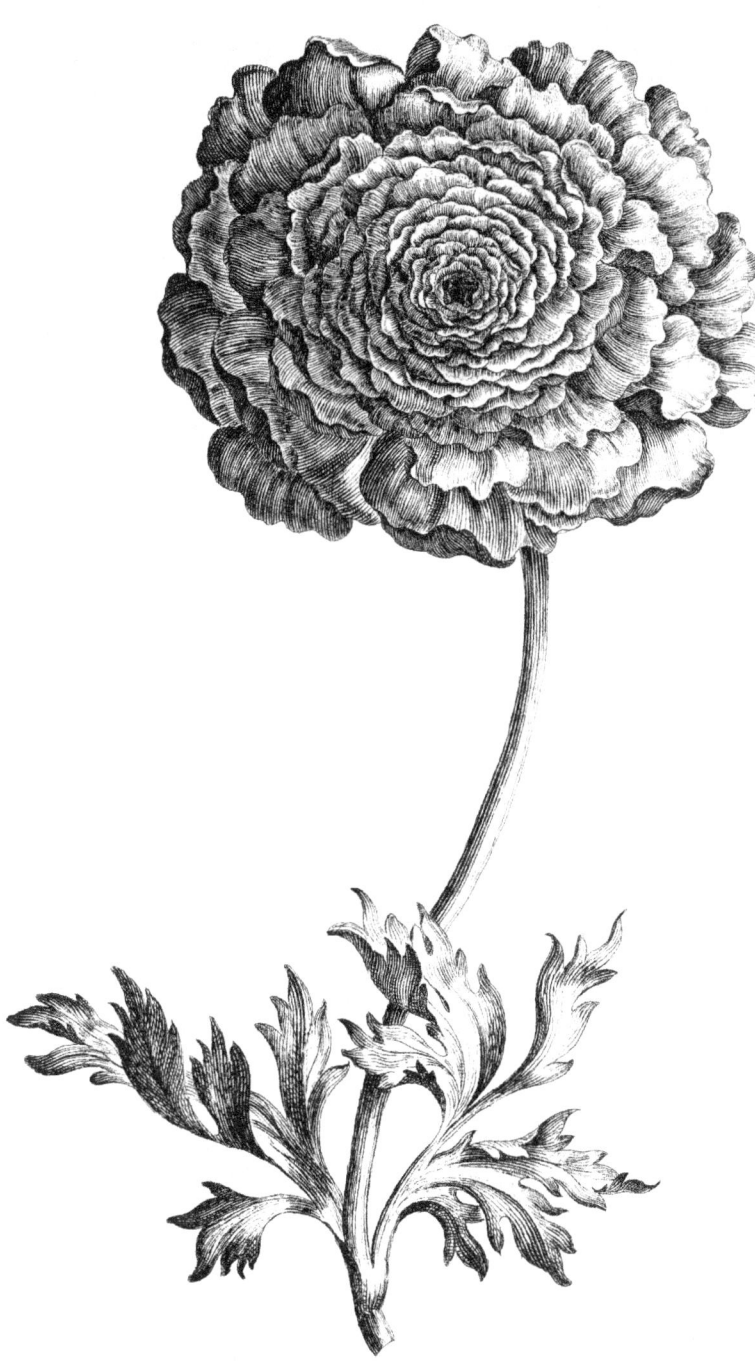

Ranuncula

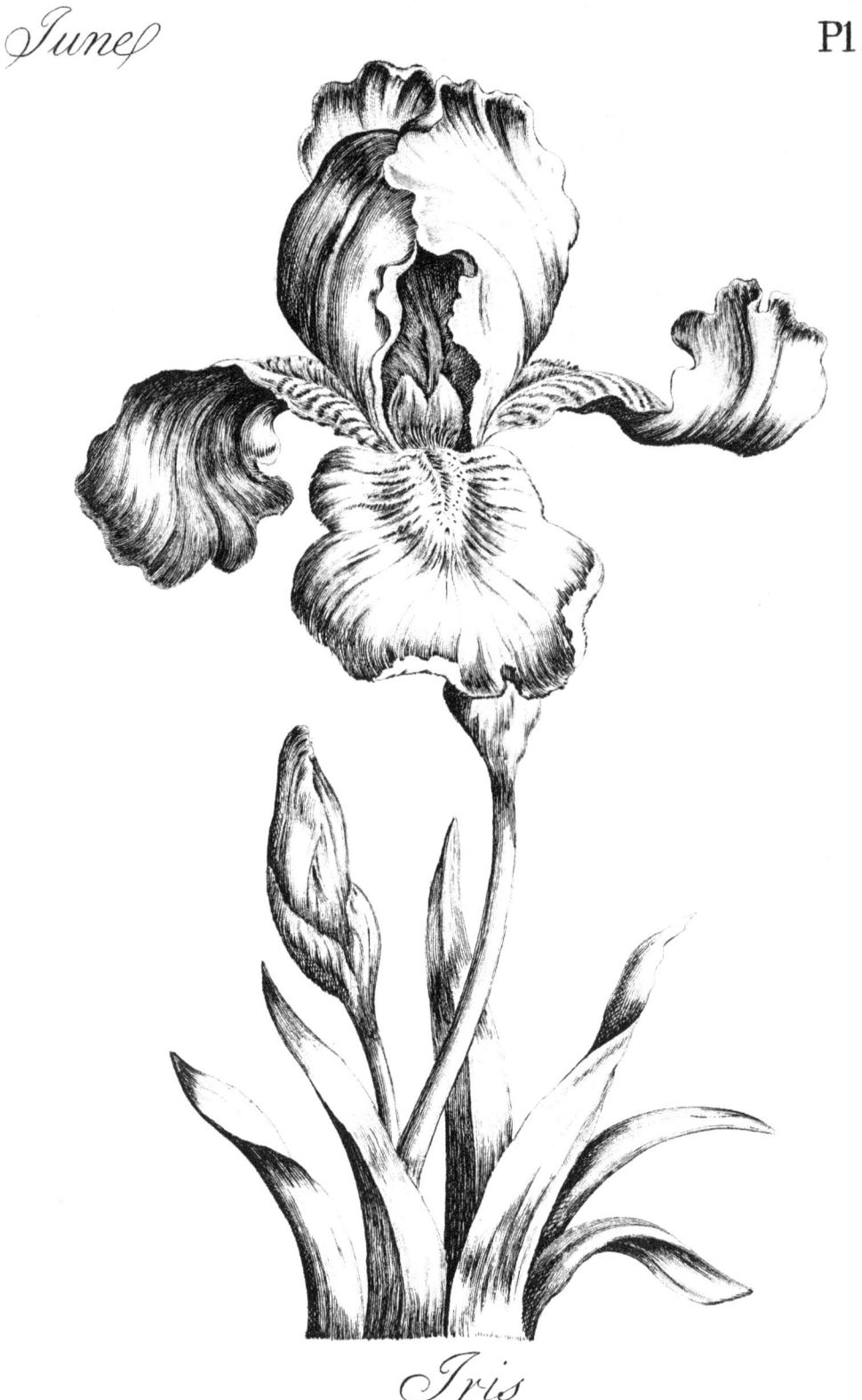

Iris

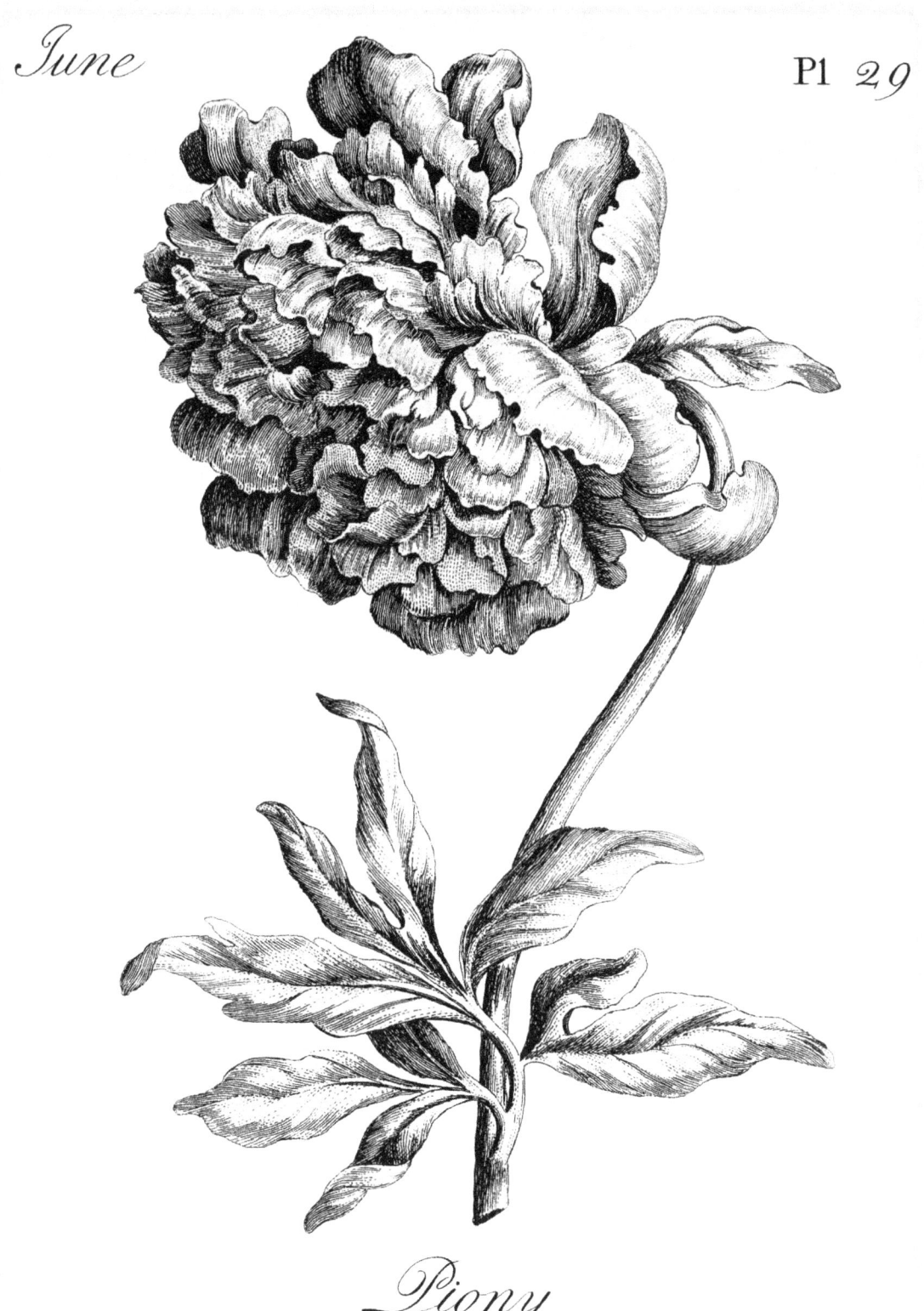

Piony

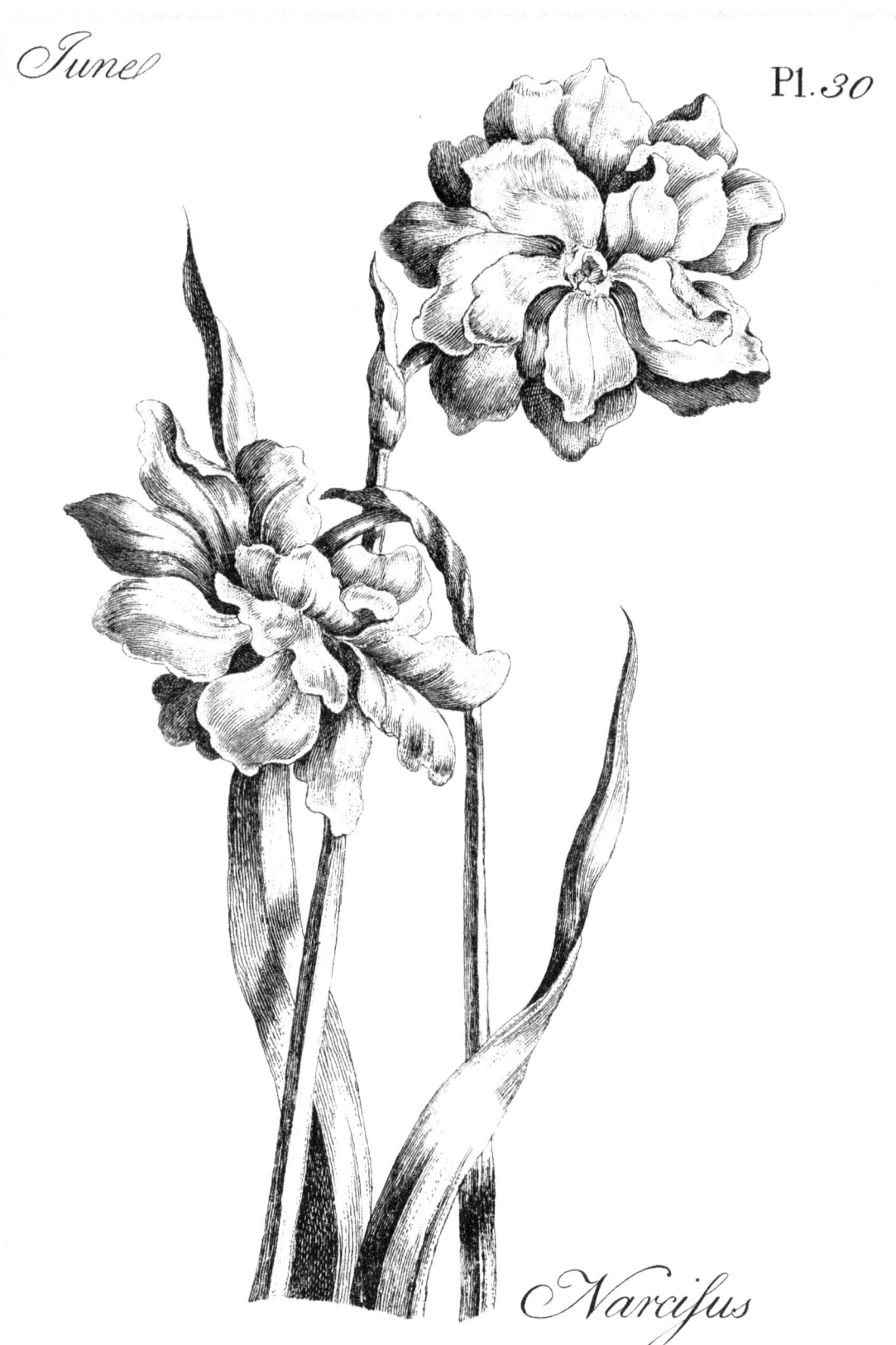

Narcisus

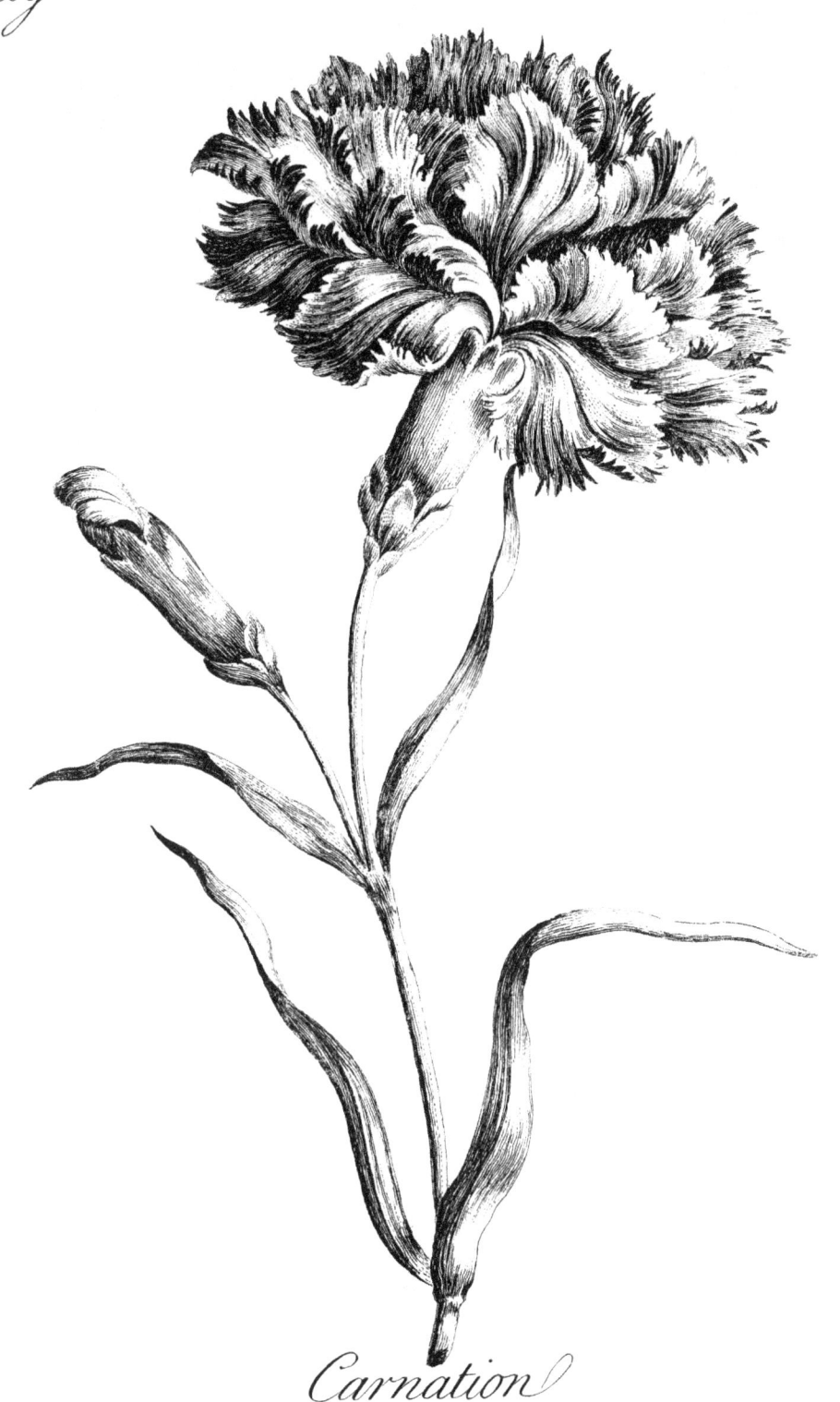

Carnation

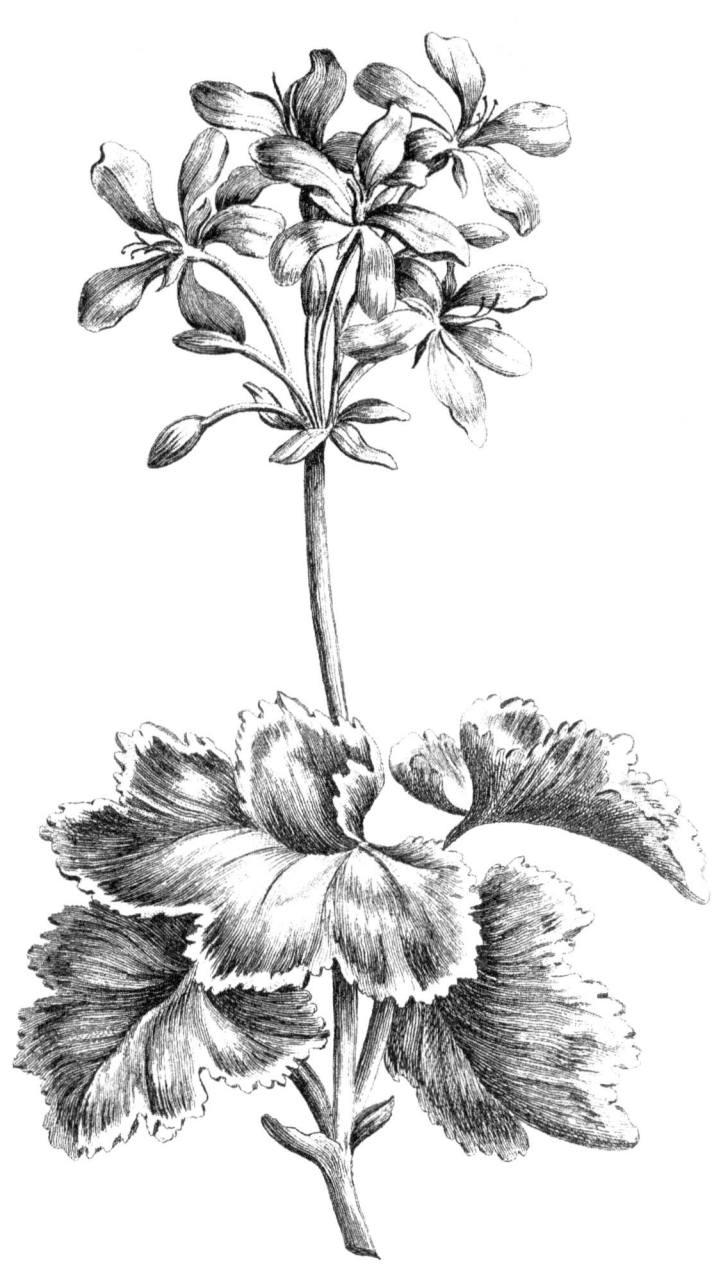

Geranium

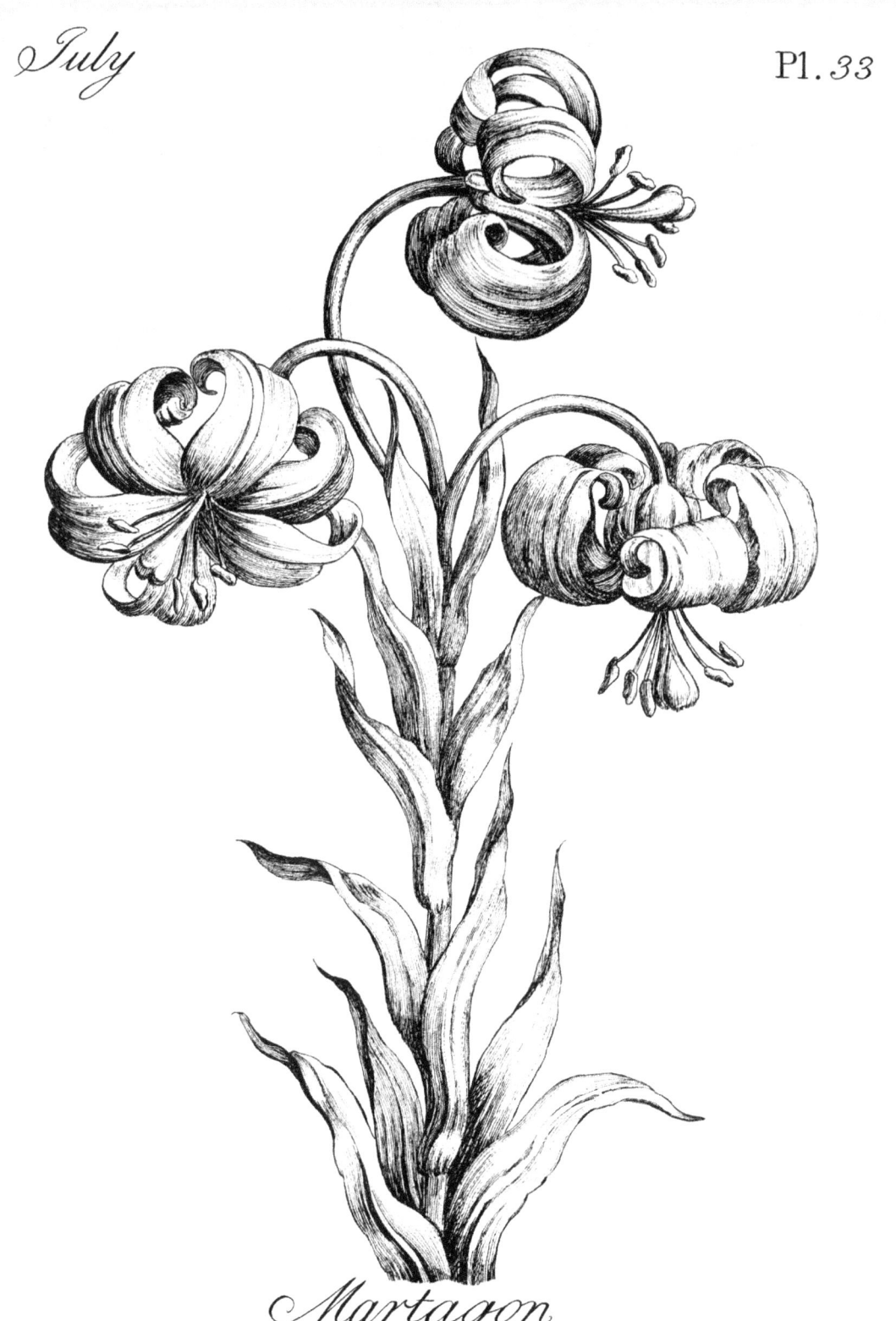

Martagon

Pl.34

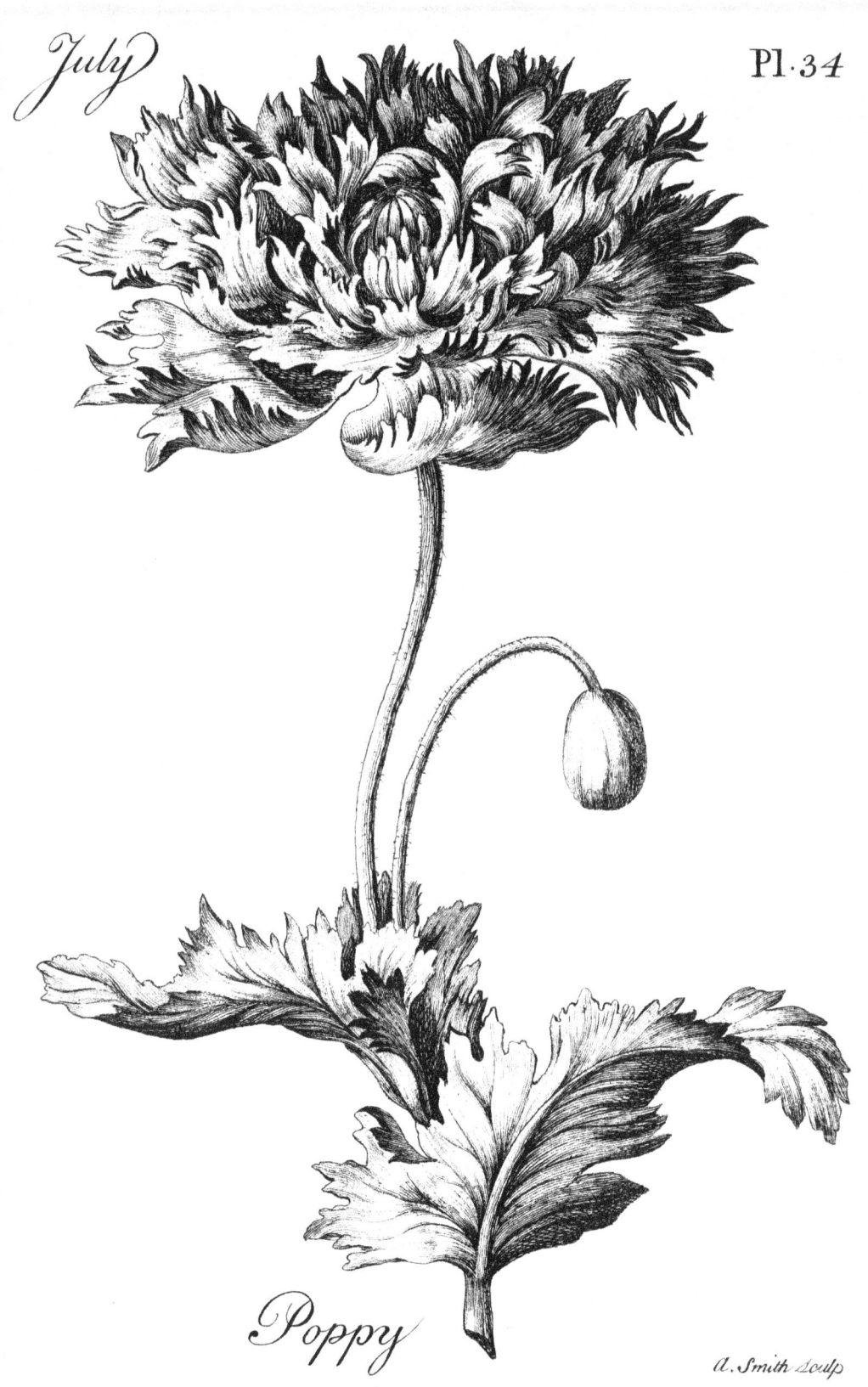

Poppy

a. Smith sculp

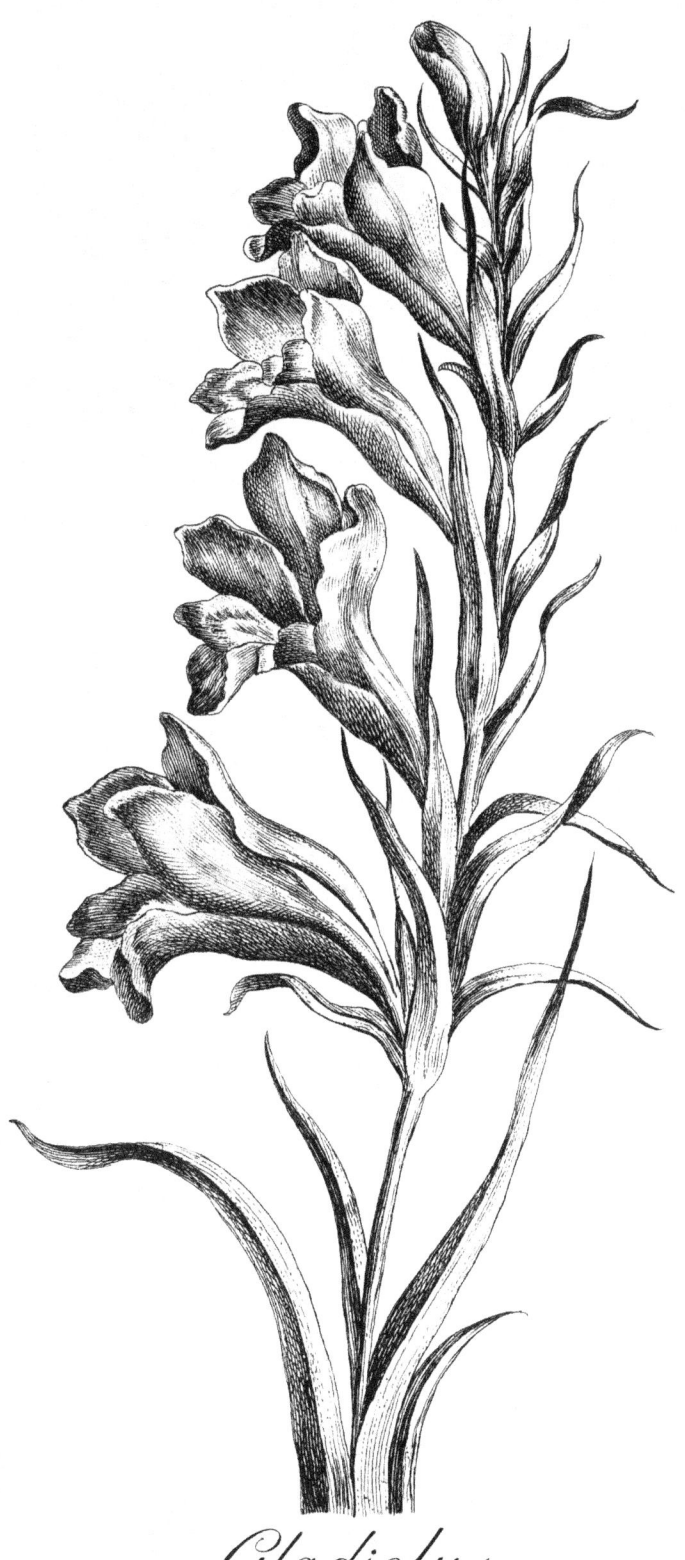

Gladiolus.

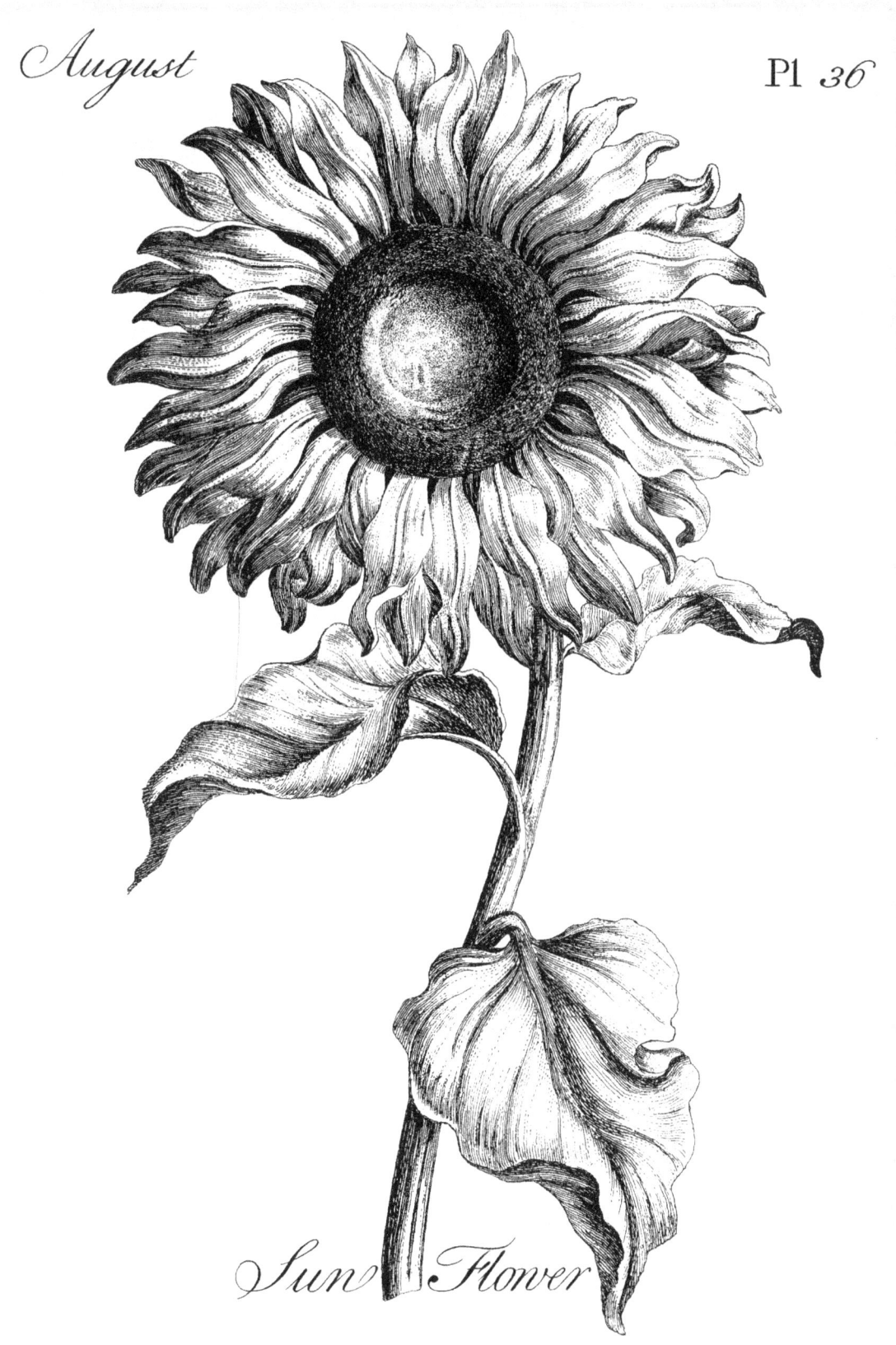

Sun Flower

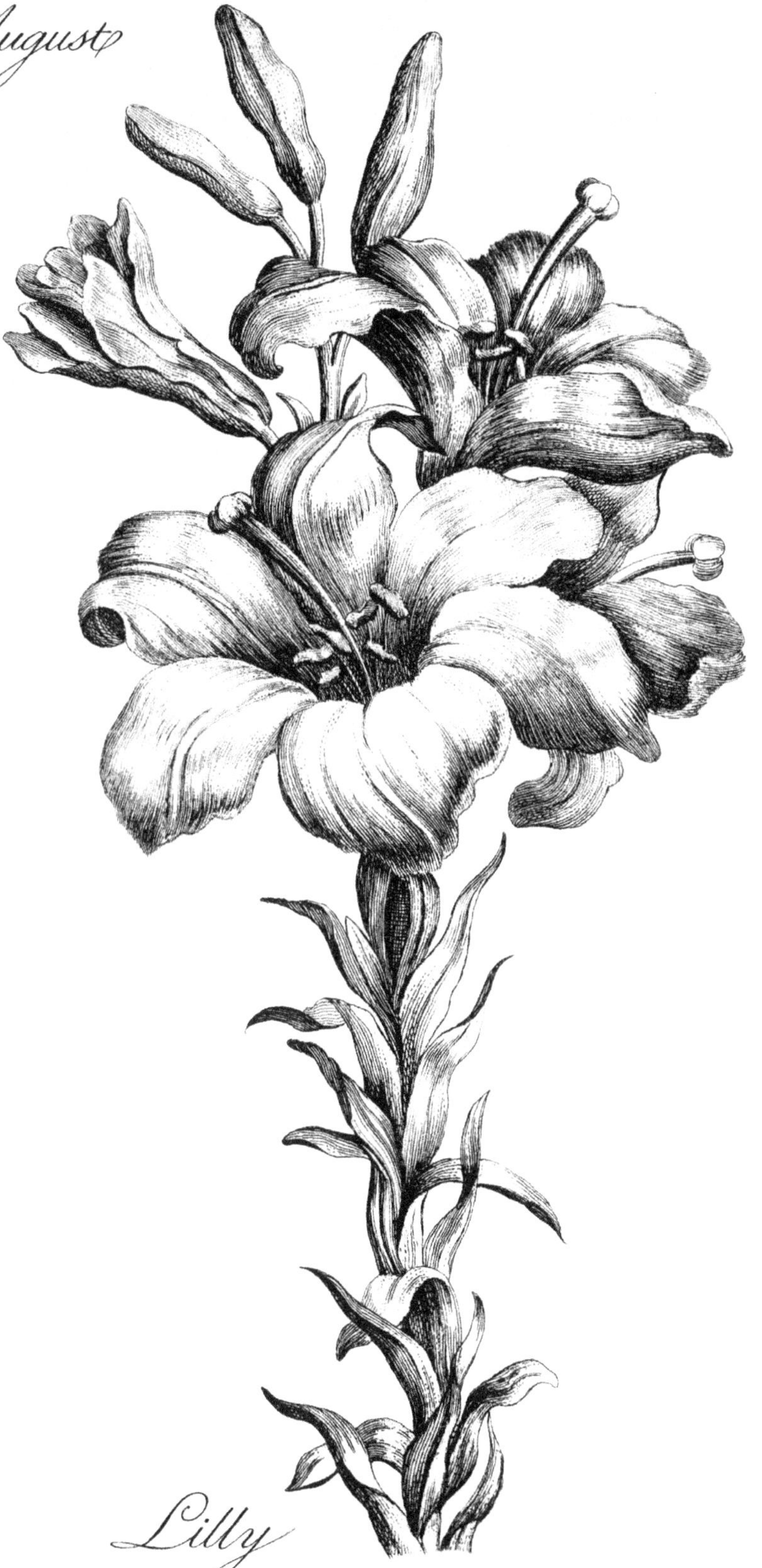

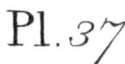

Lilly

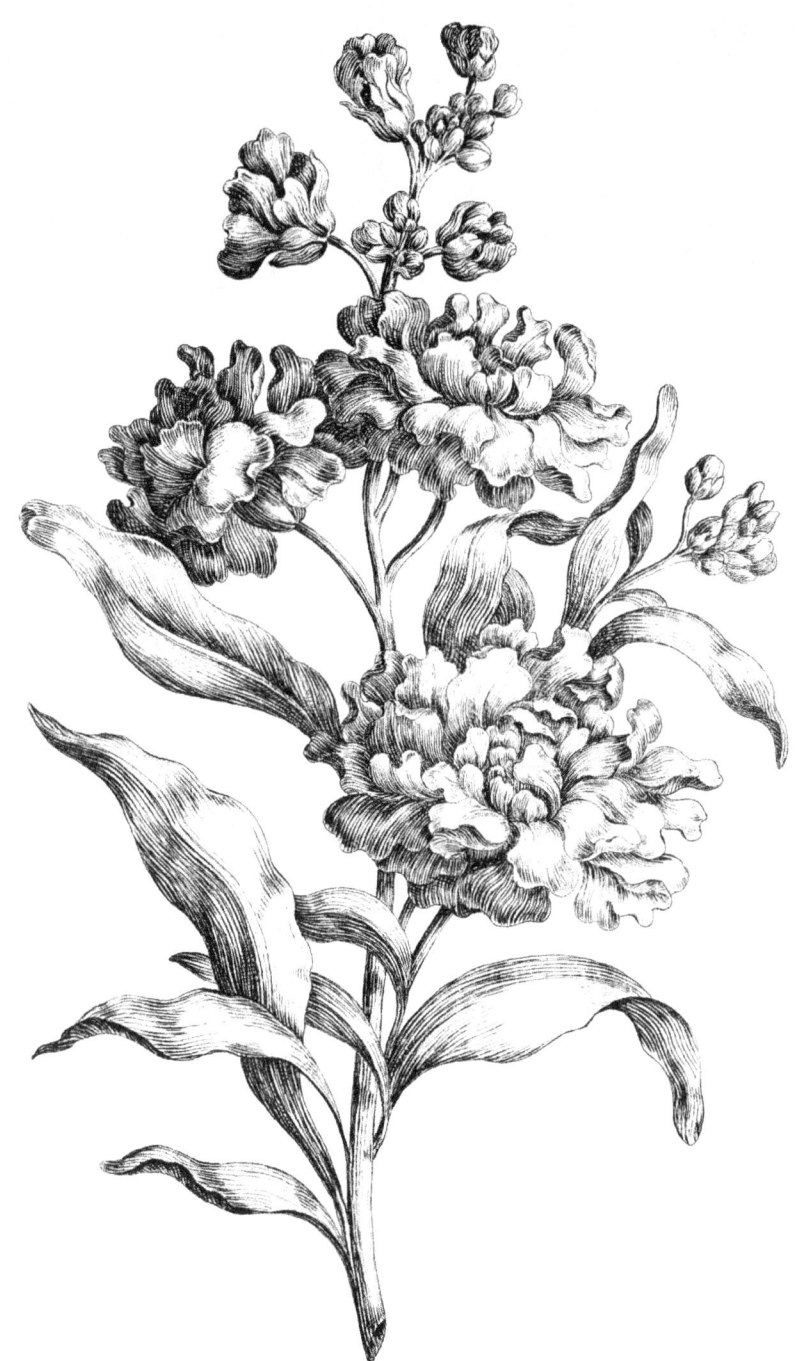

Double Stock

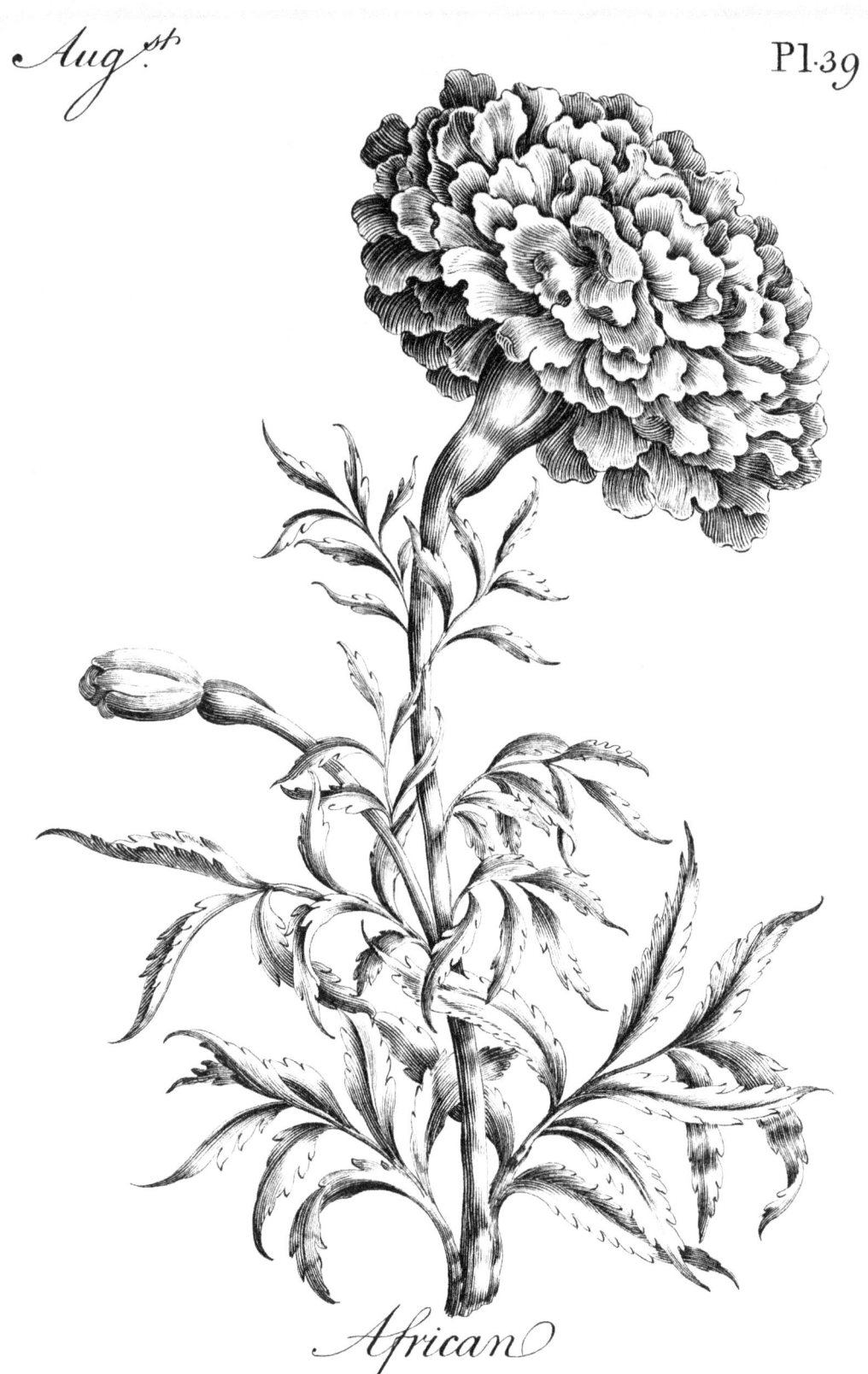

African

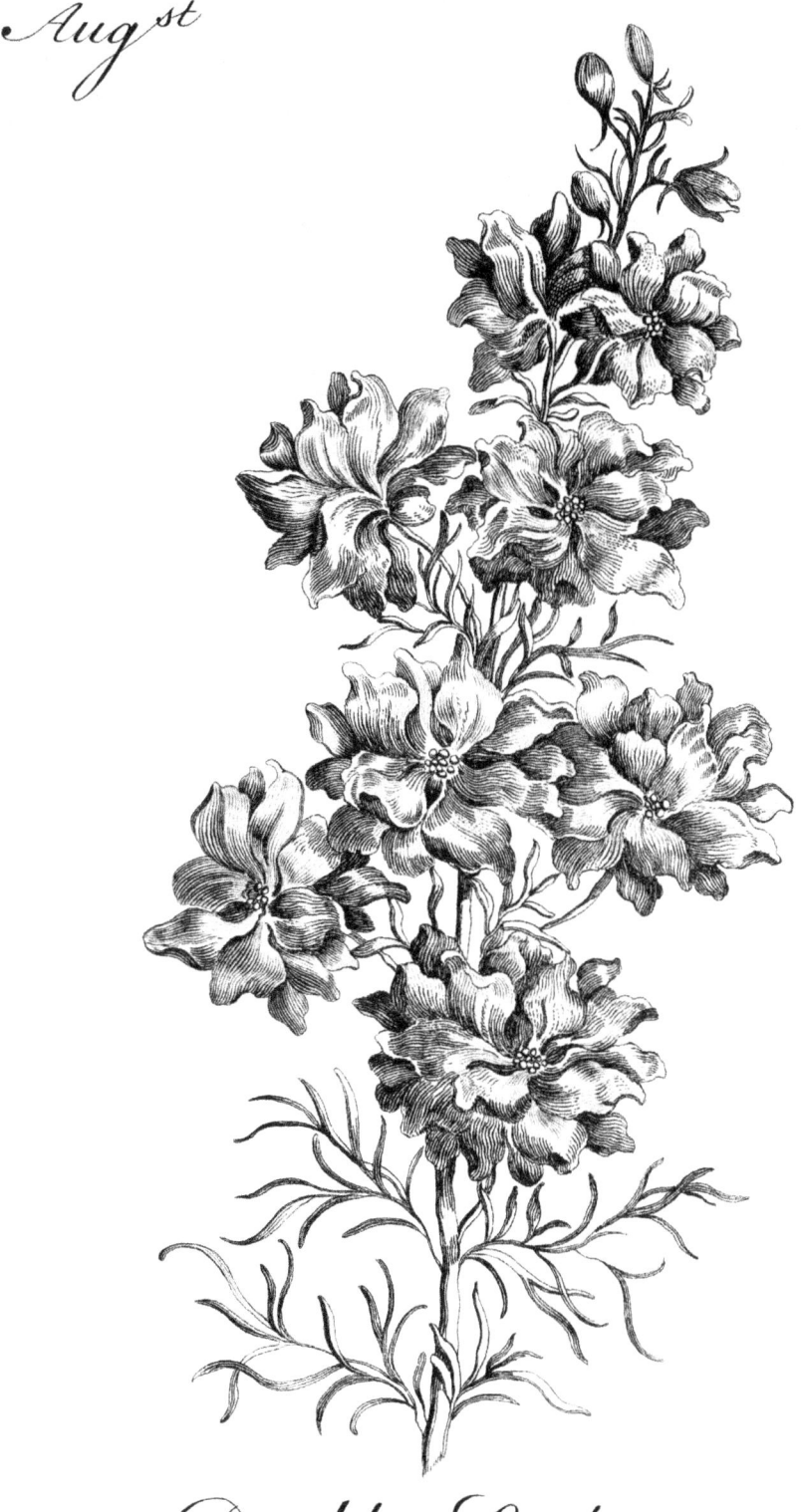

Double Larkspur

Pl. 41

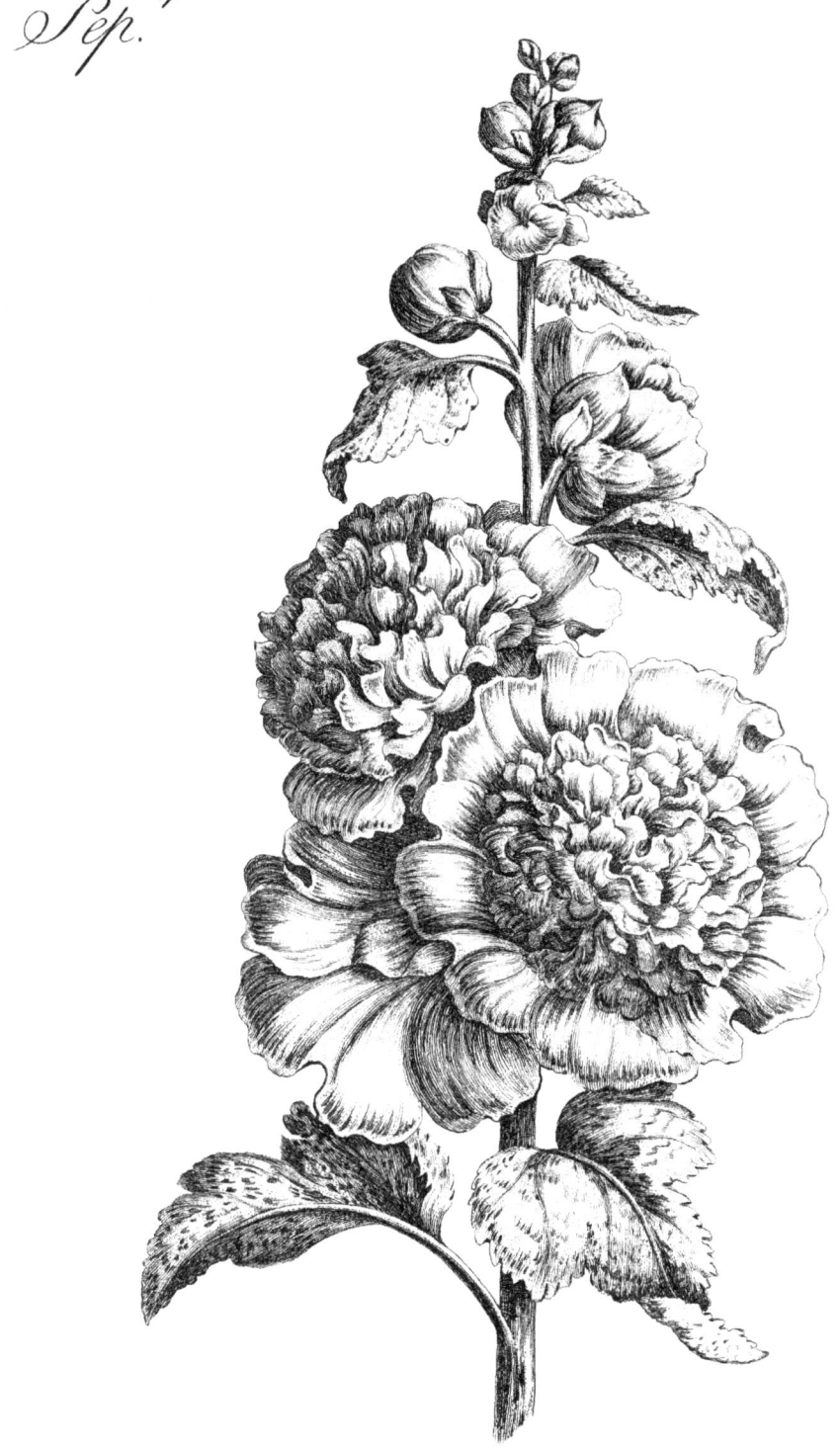

Hollyhock

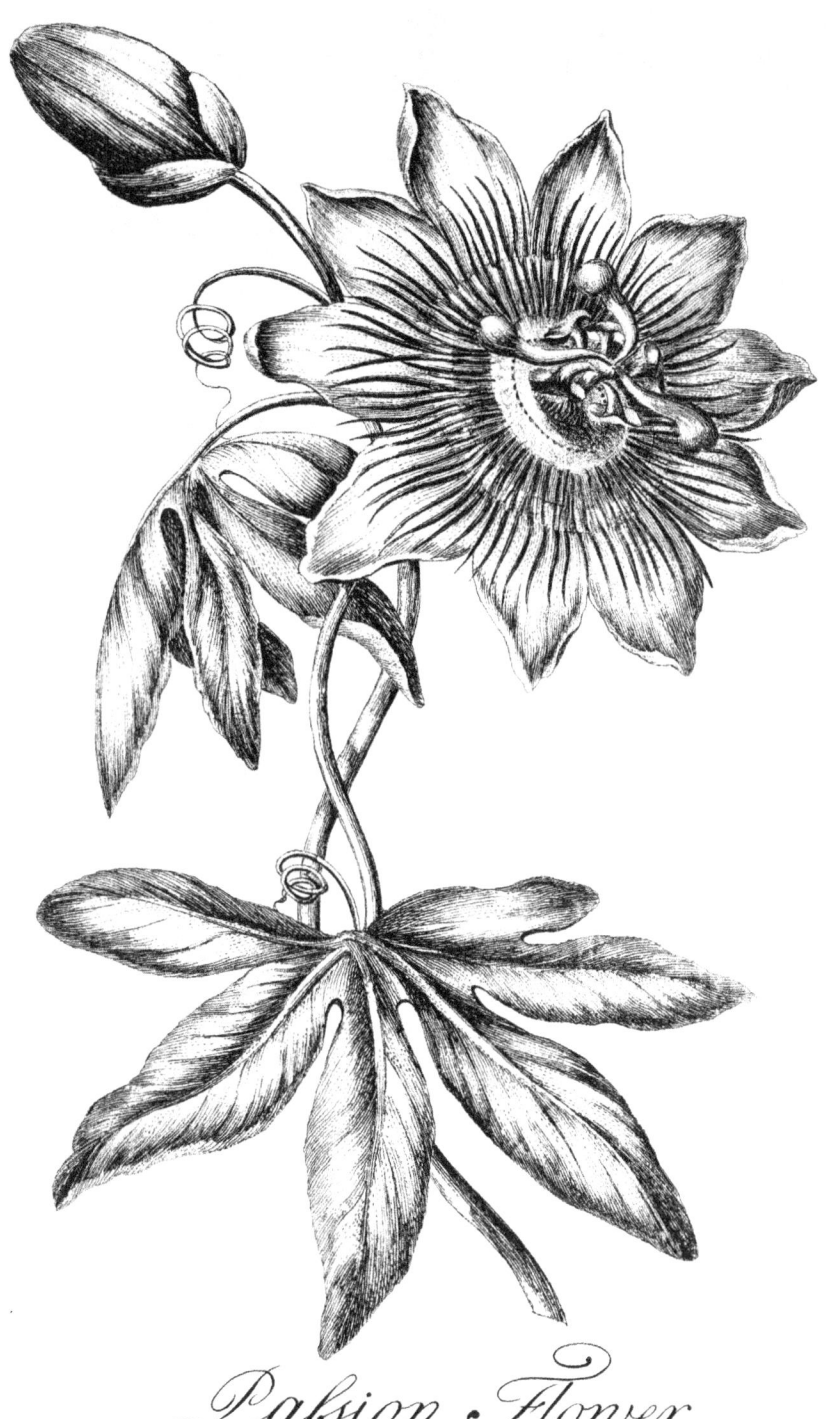

Passion Flower

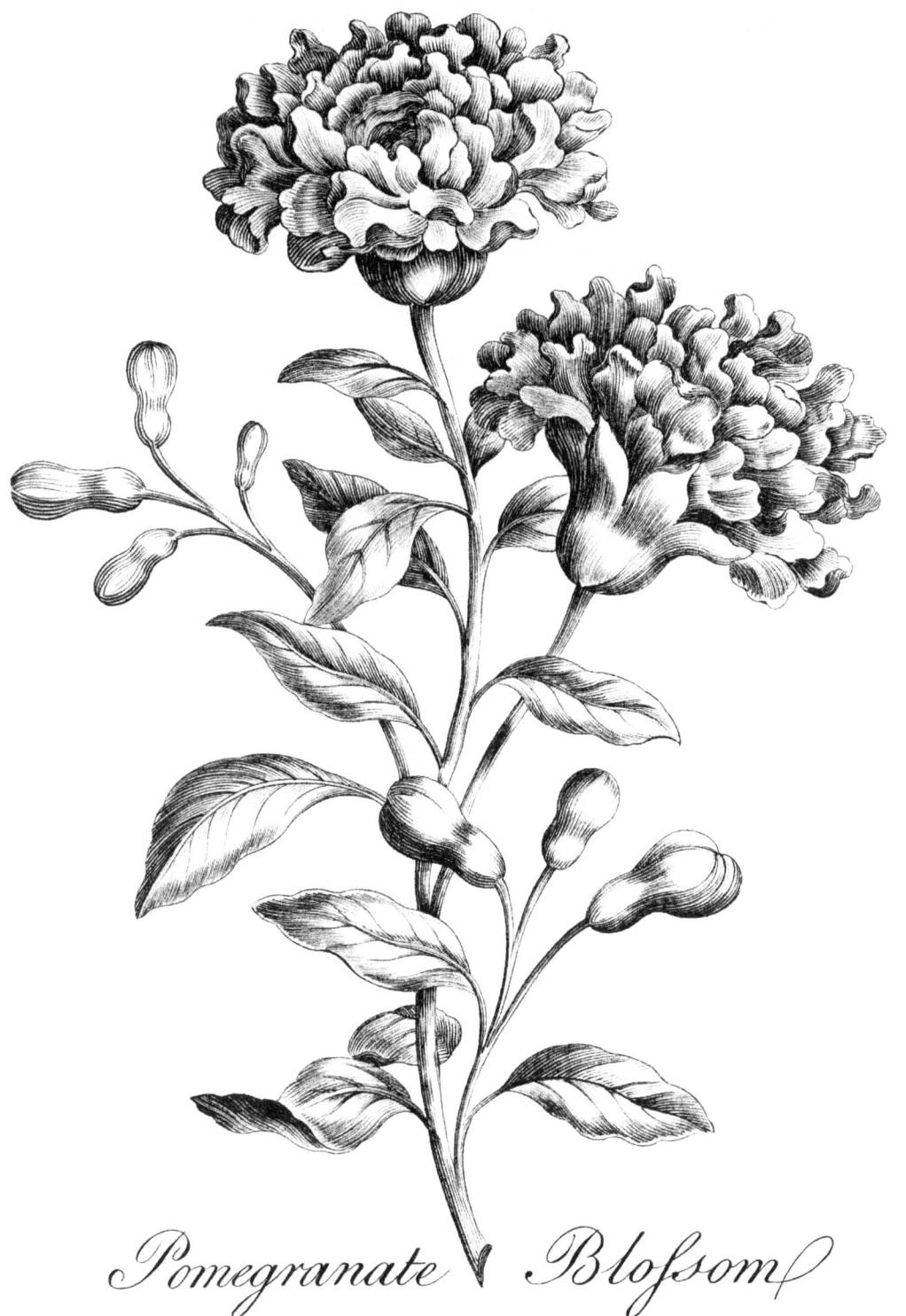

Pomegranate Blossom

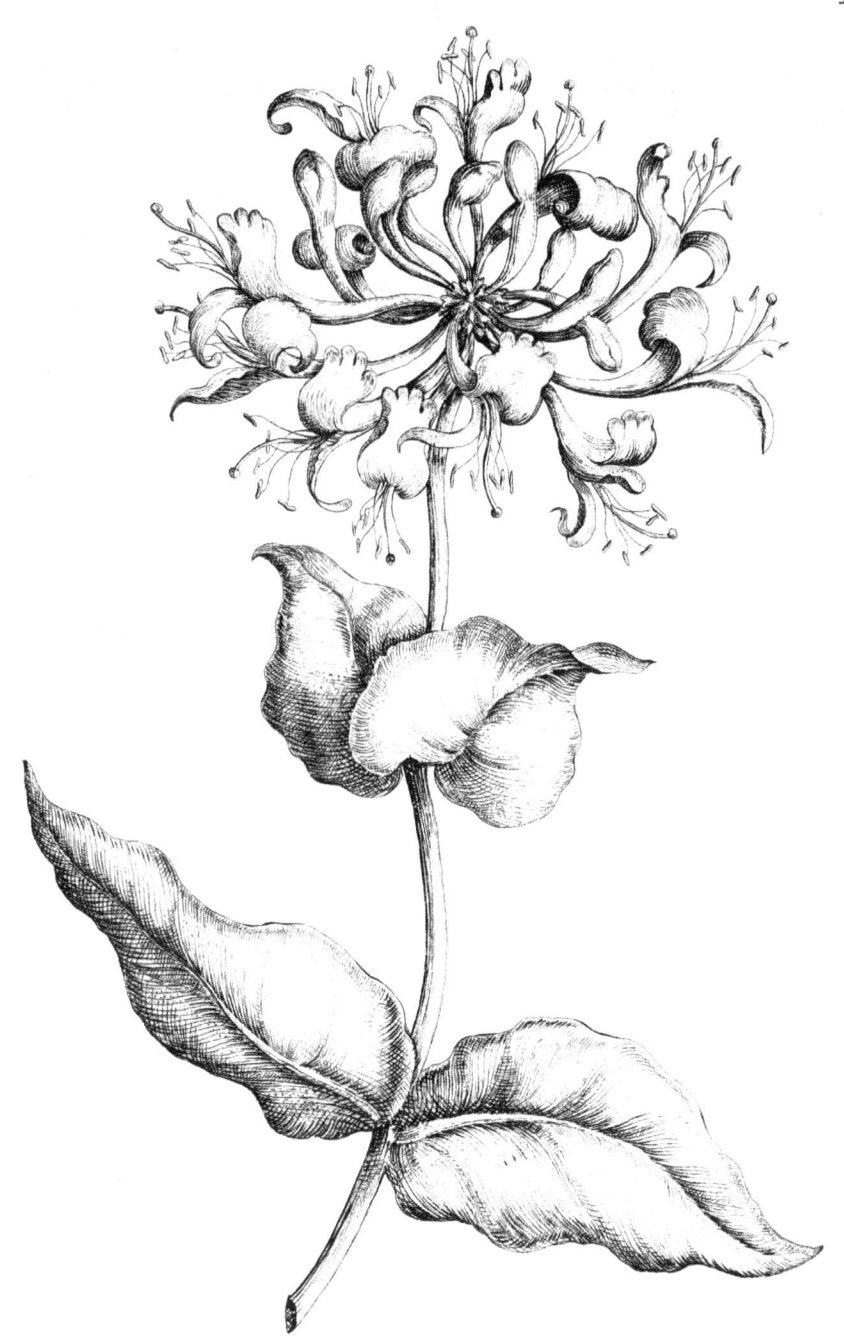

Honeysuckle

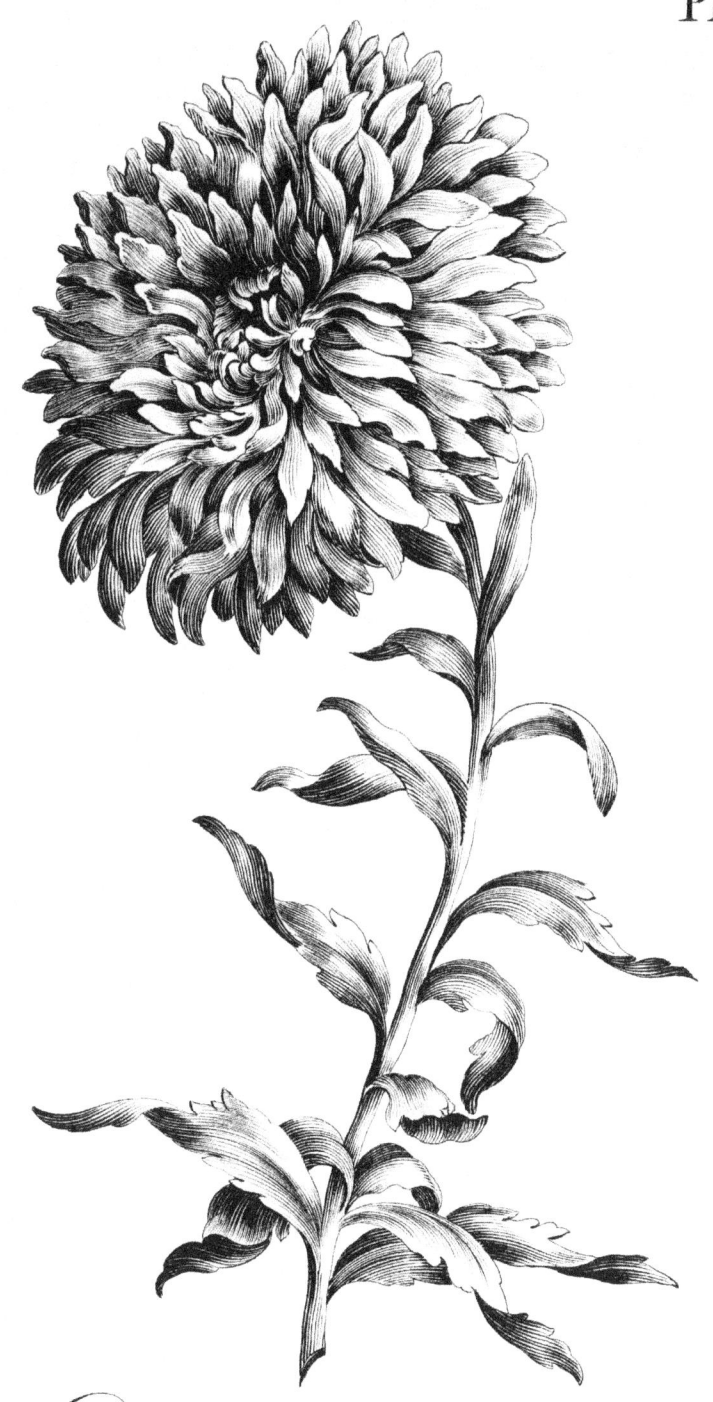

Double China Aster.

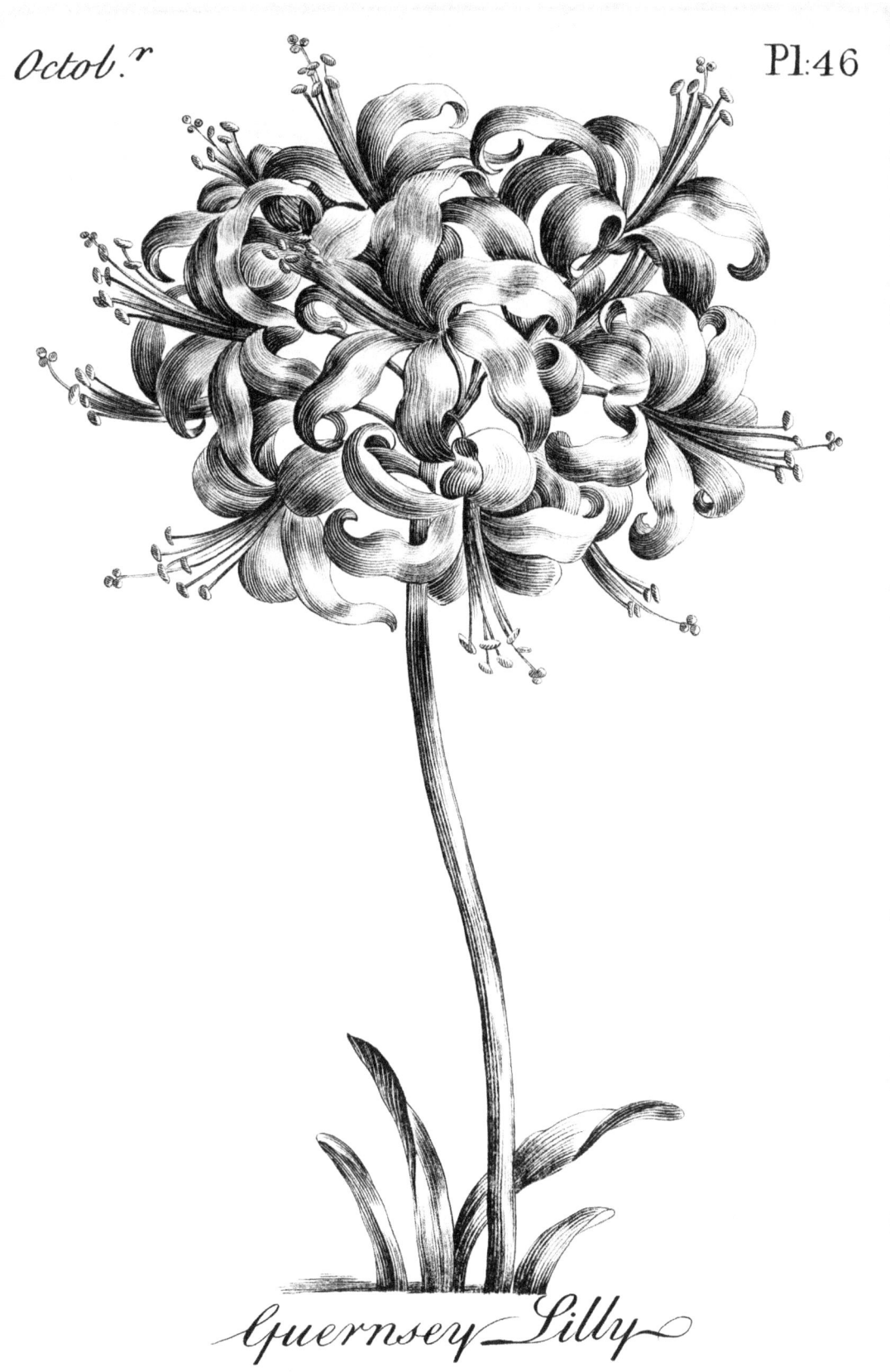

Guernsey Lilly

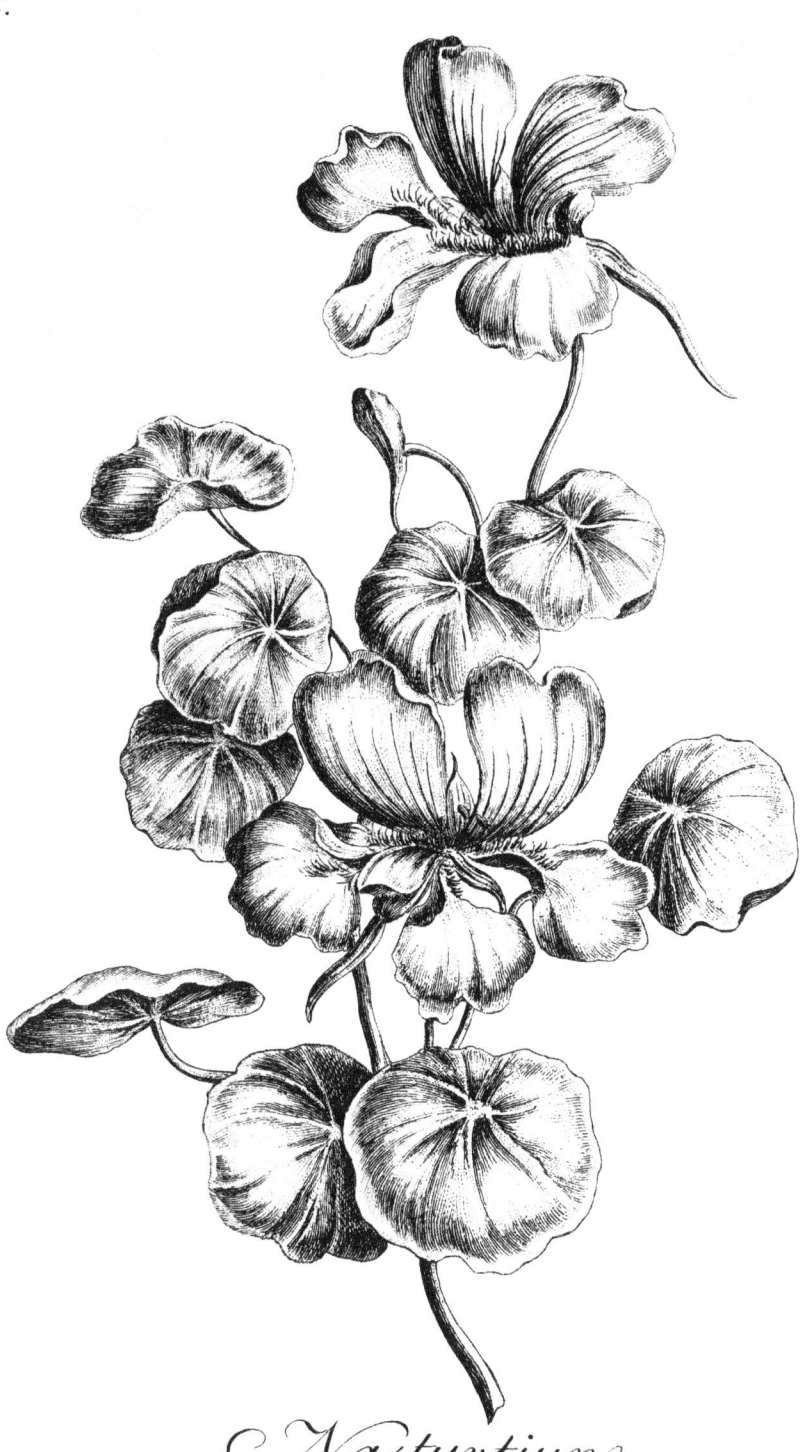

Nasturtiun

Pl. 48

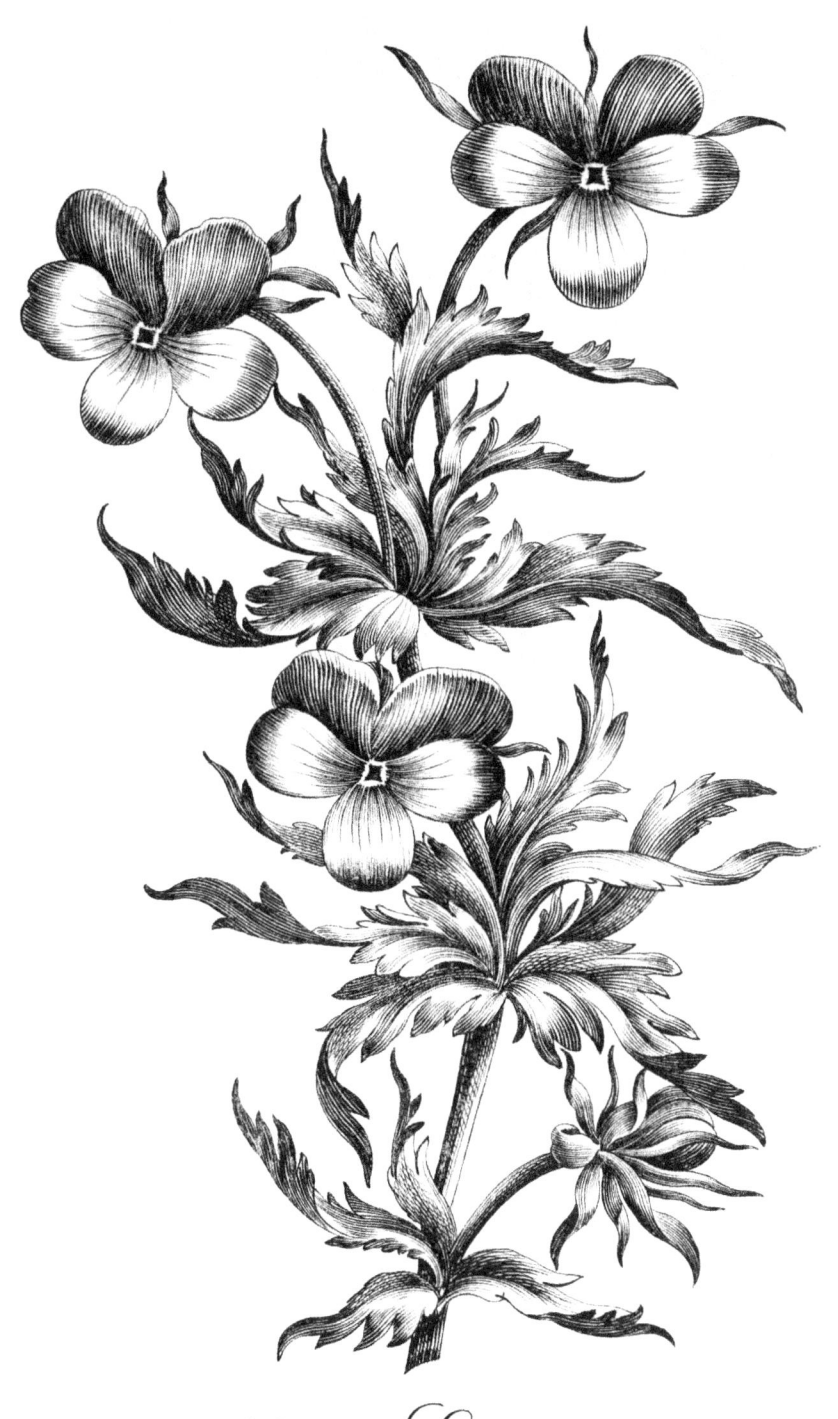

Heart's Ease

Pl.49

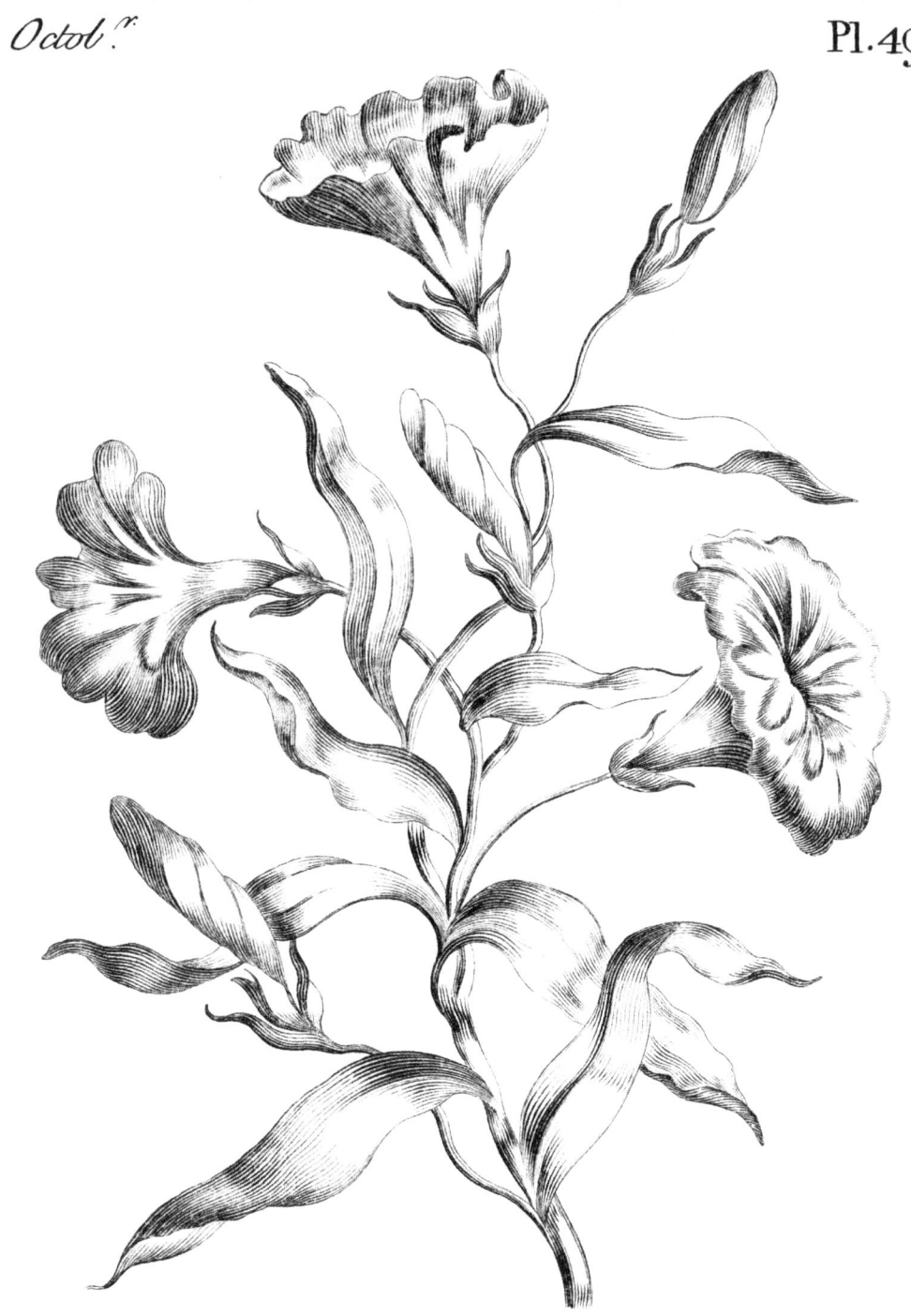

Convolvulus

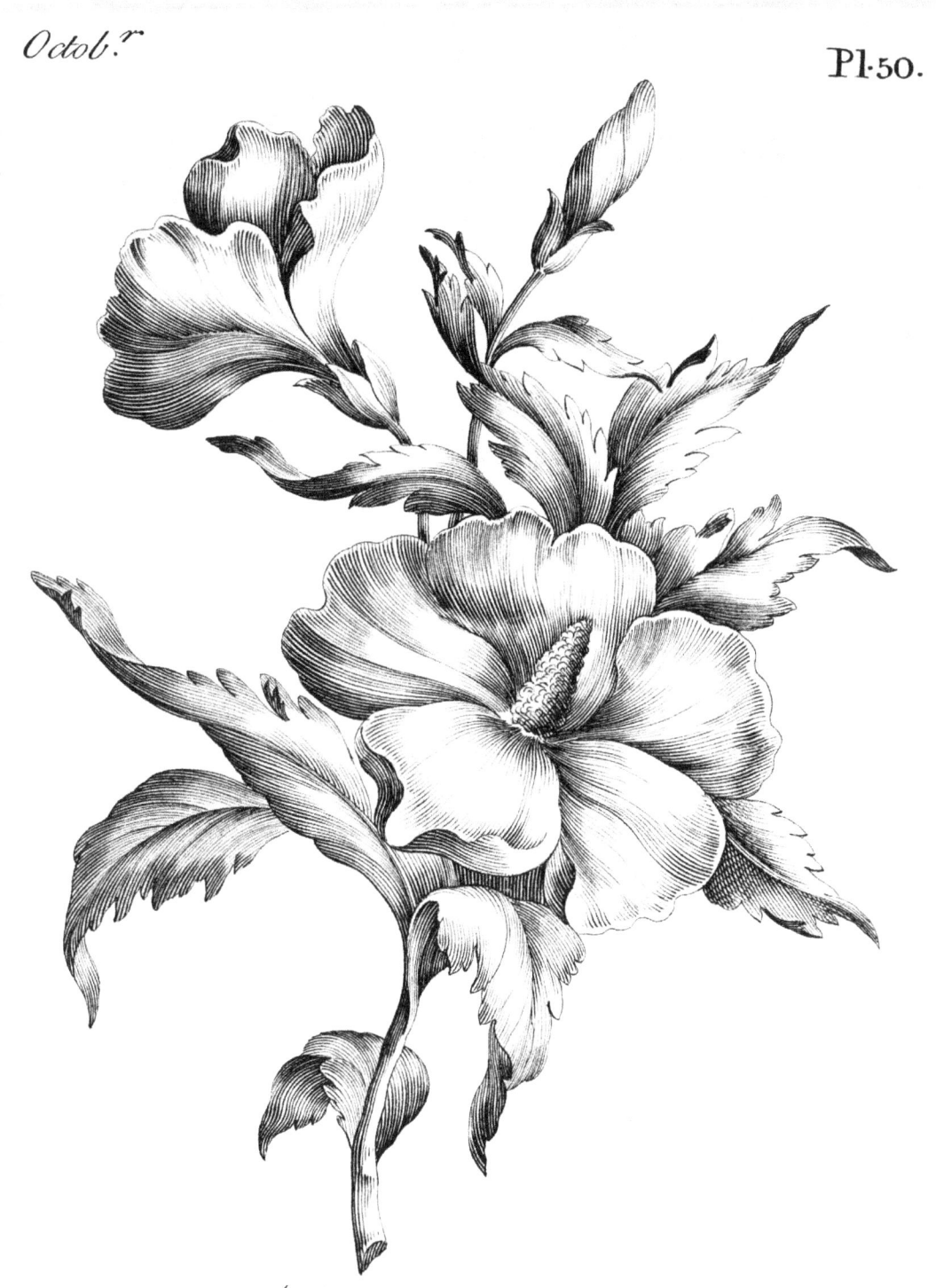

Athæa Frutex.

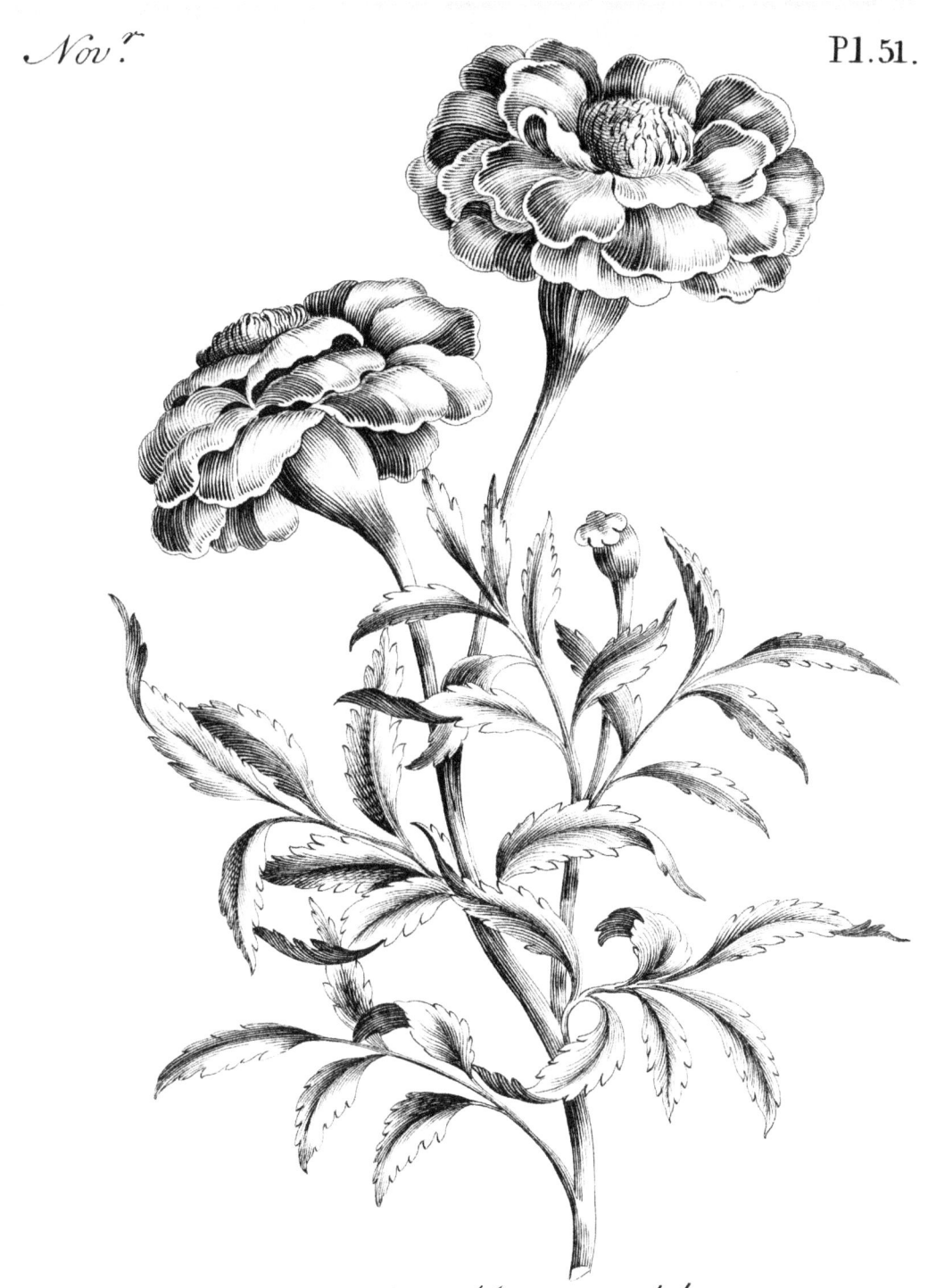

French Marygold

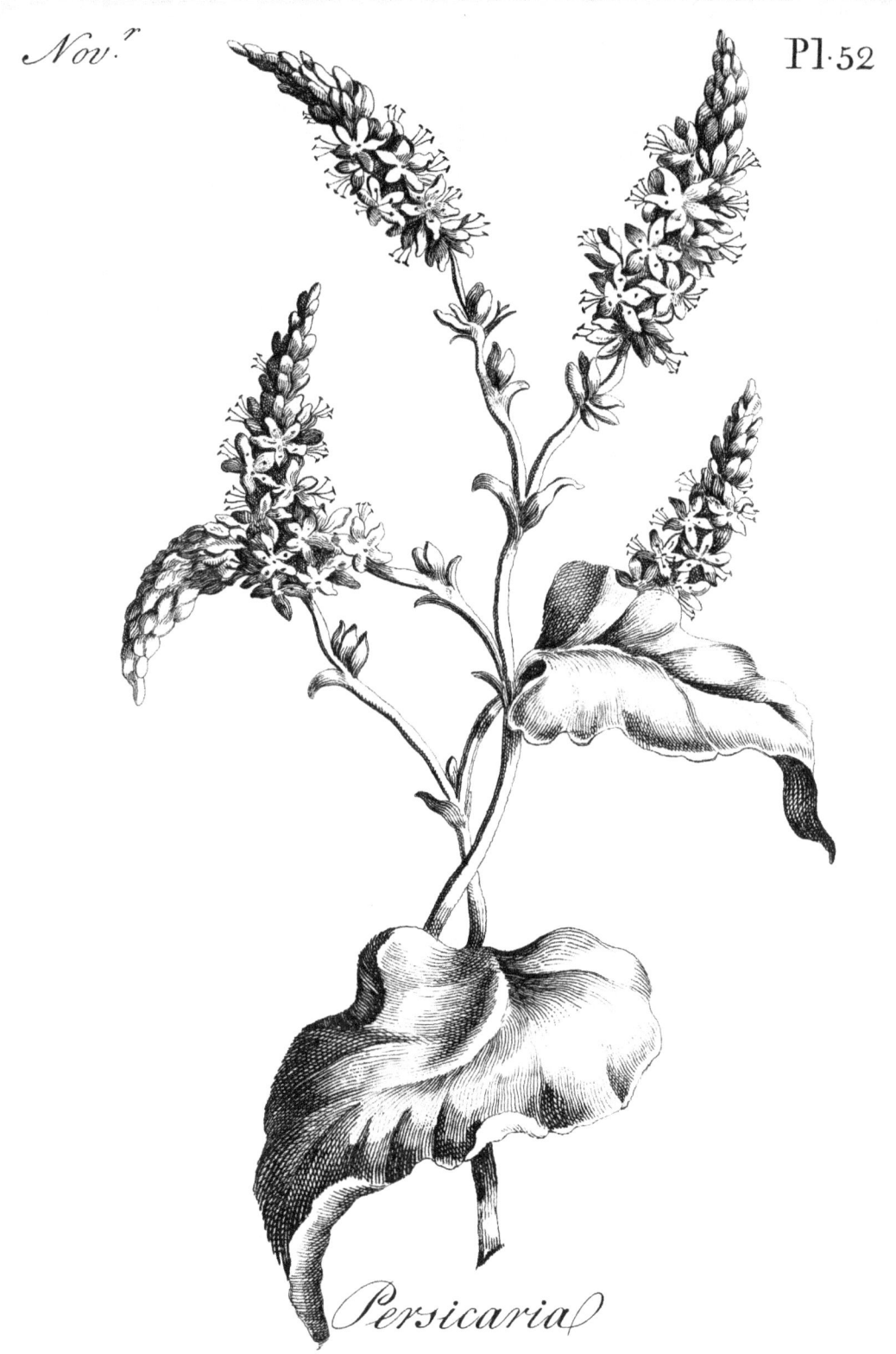

Persicaria

Pl. 53

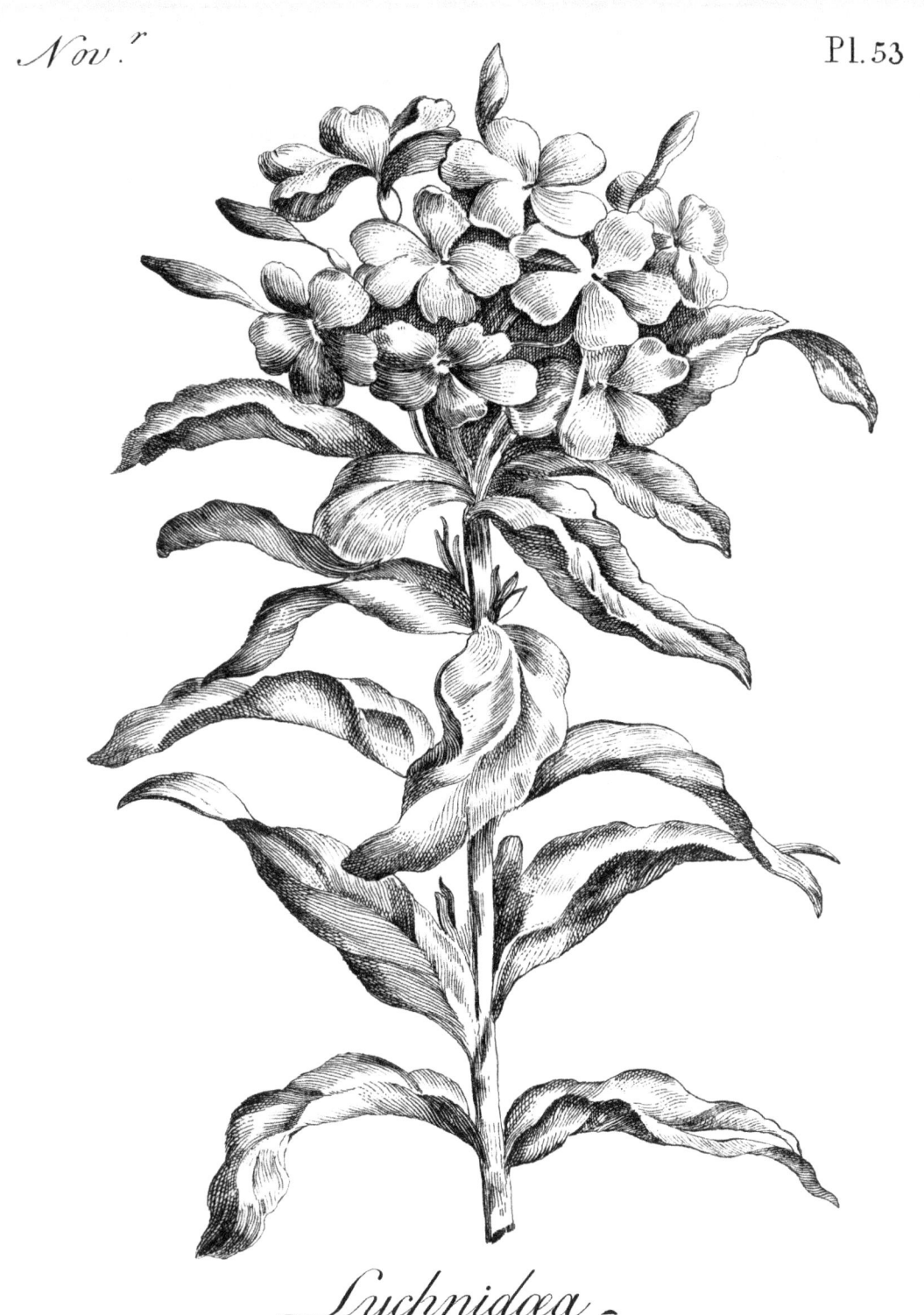

Lychnidœa.

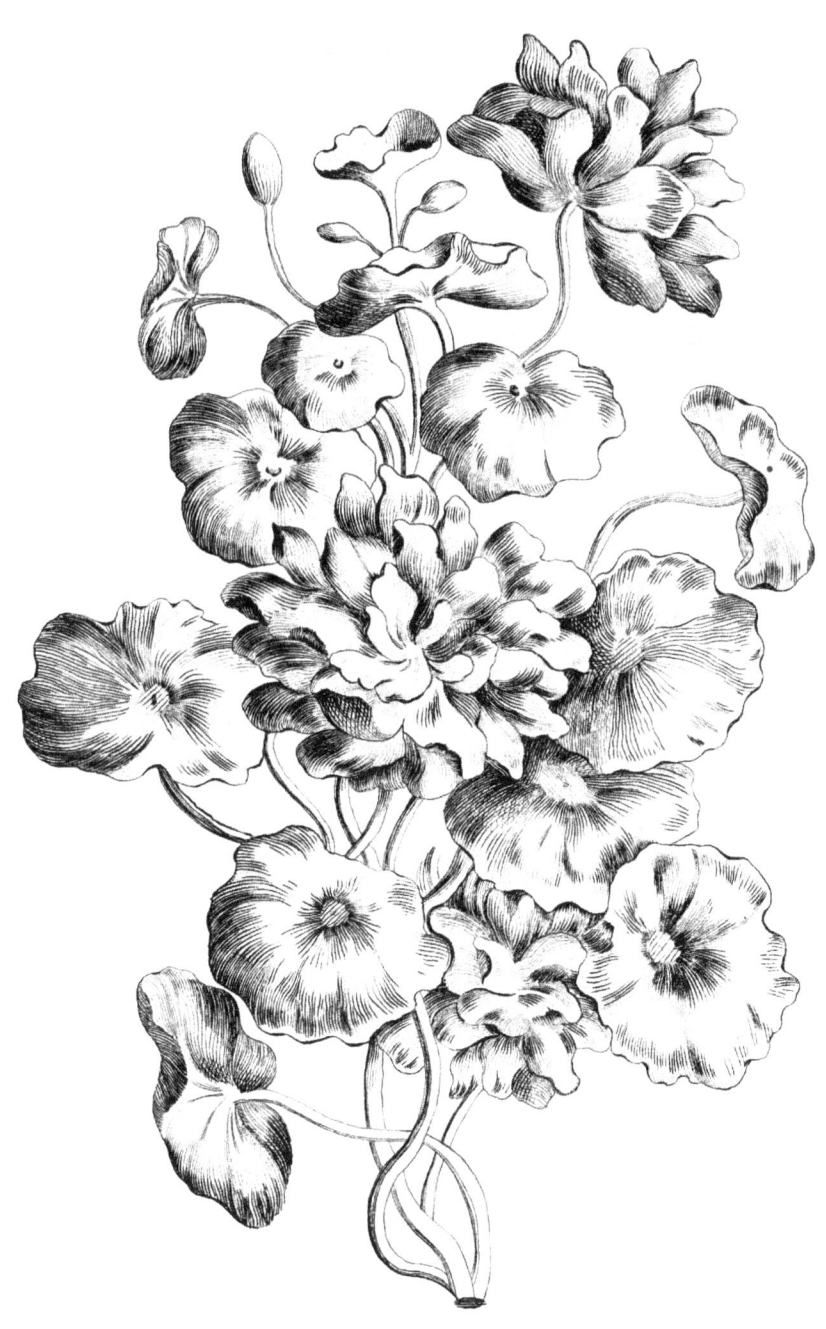

Double Nasturtian

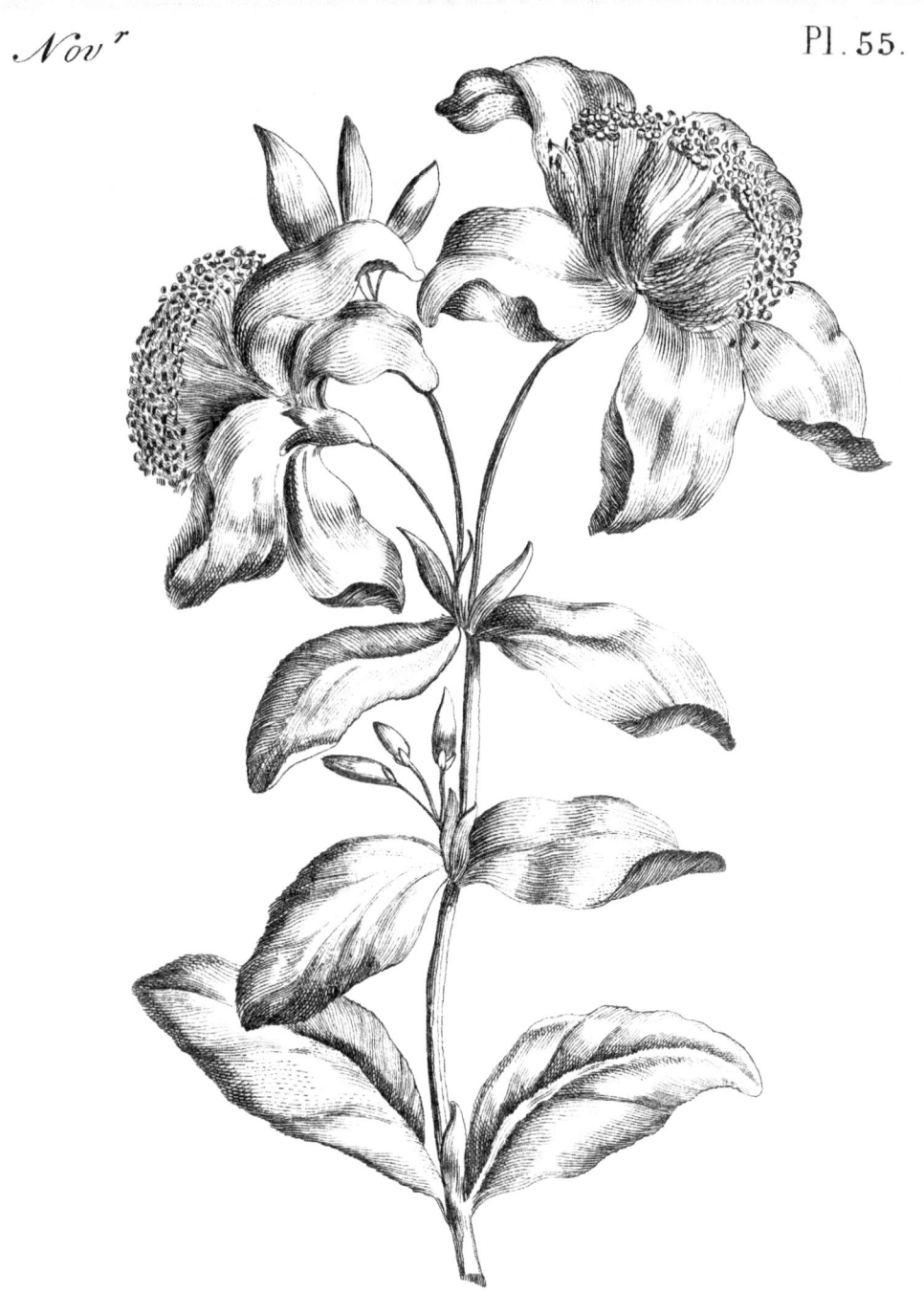

St John's Wort

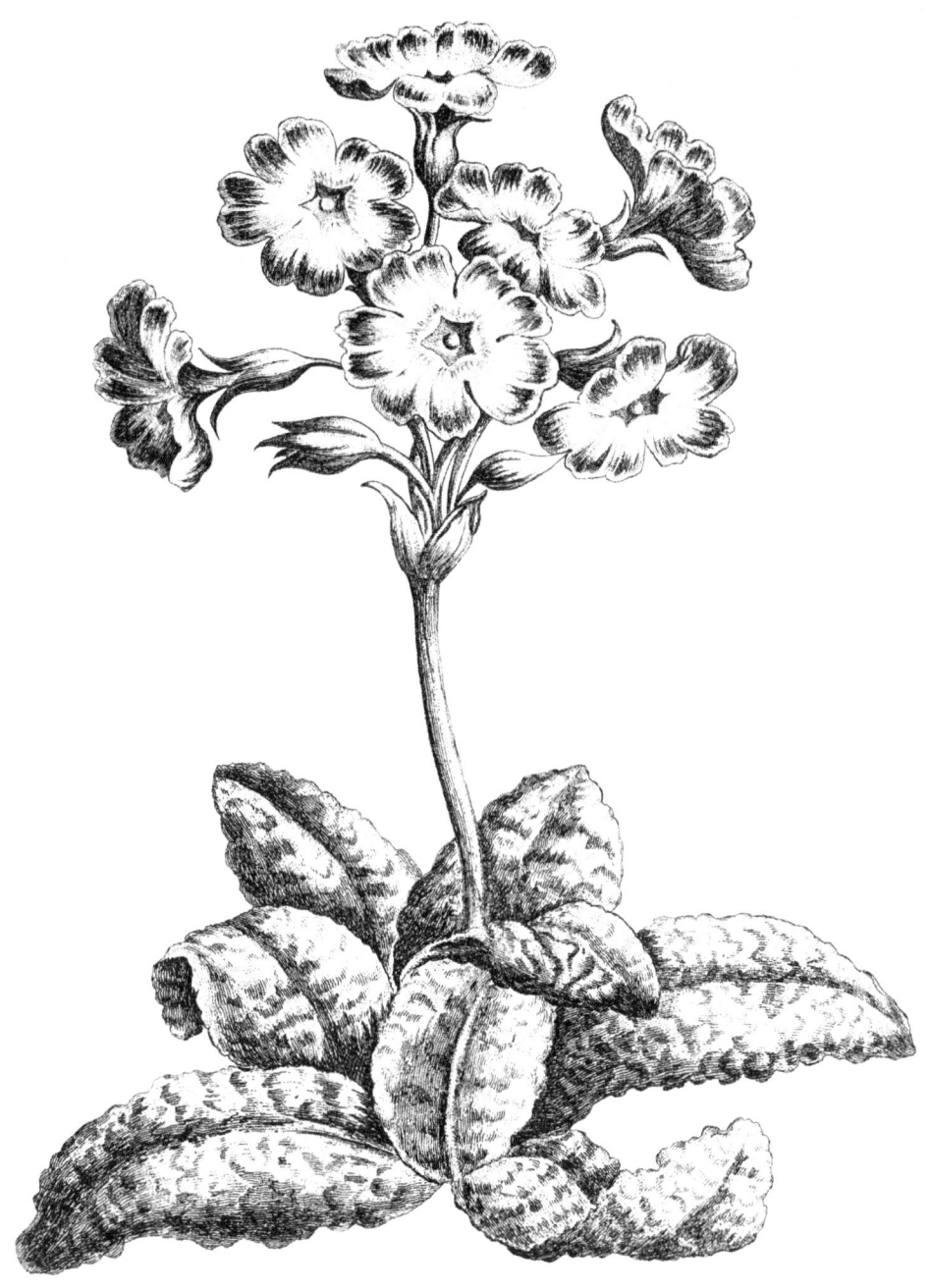

Polianthus

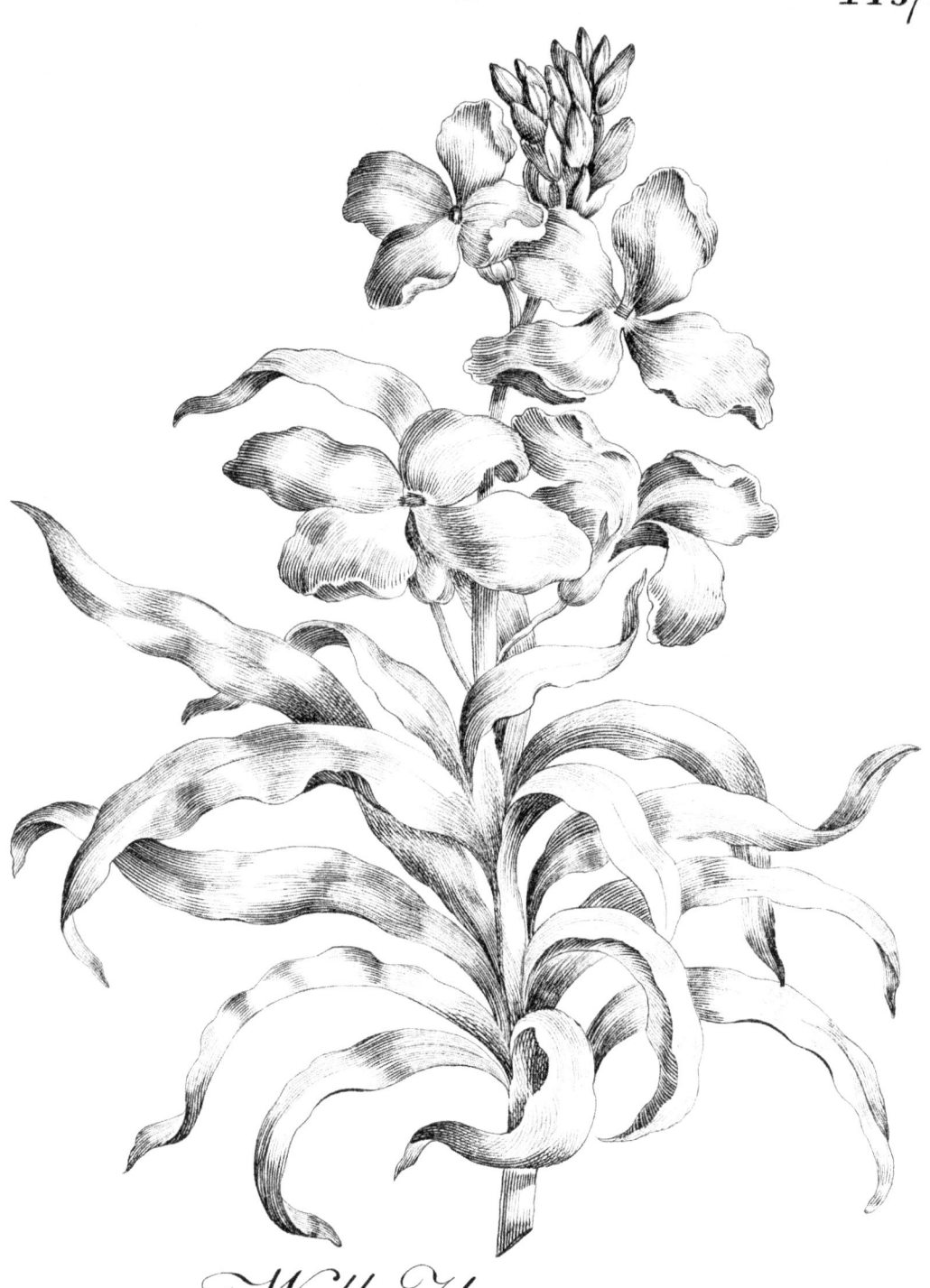

Wall Flower.

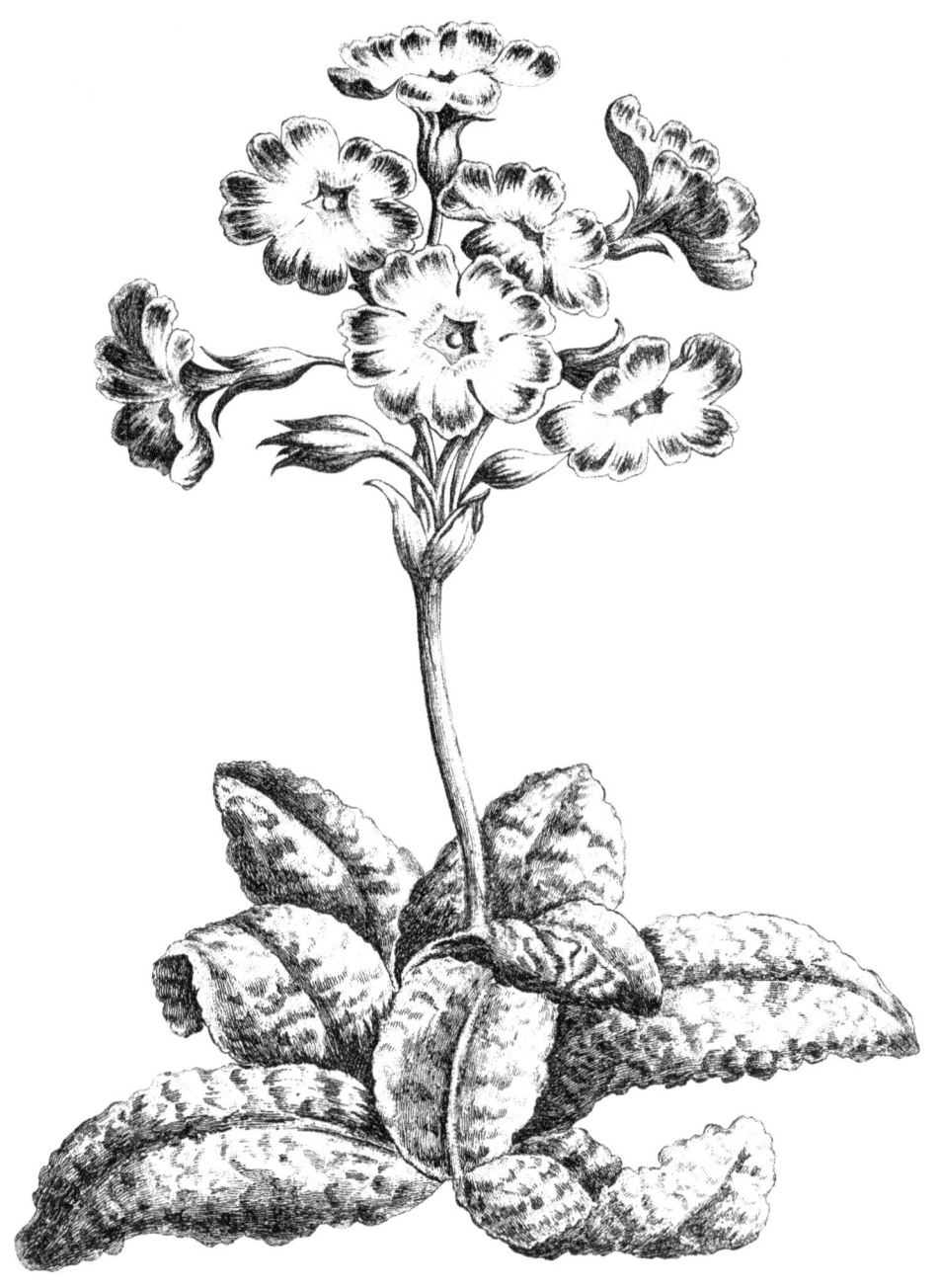

Polianthus

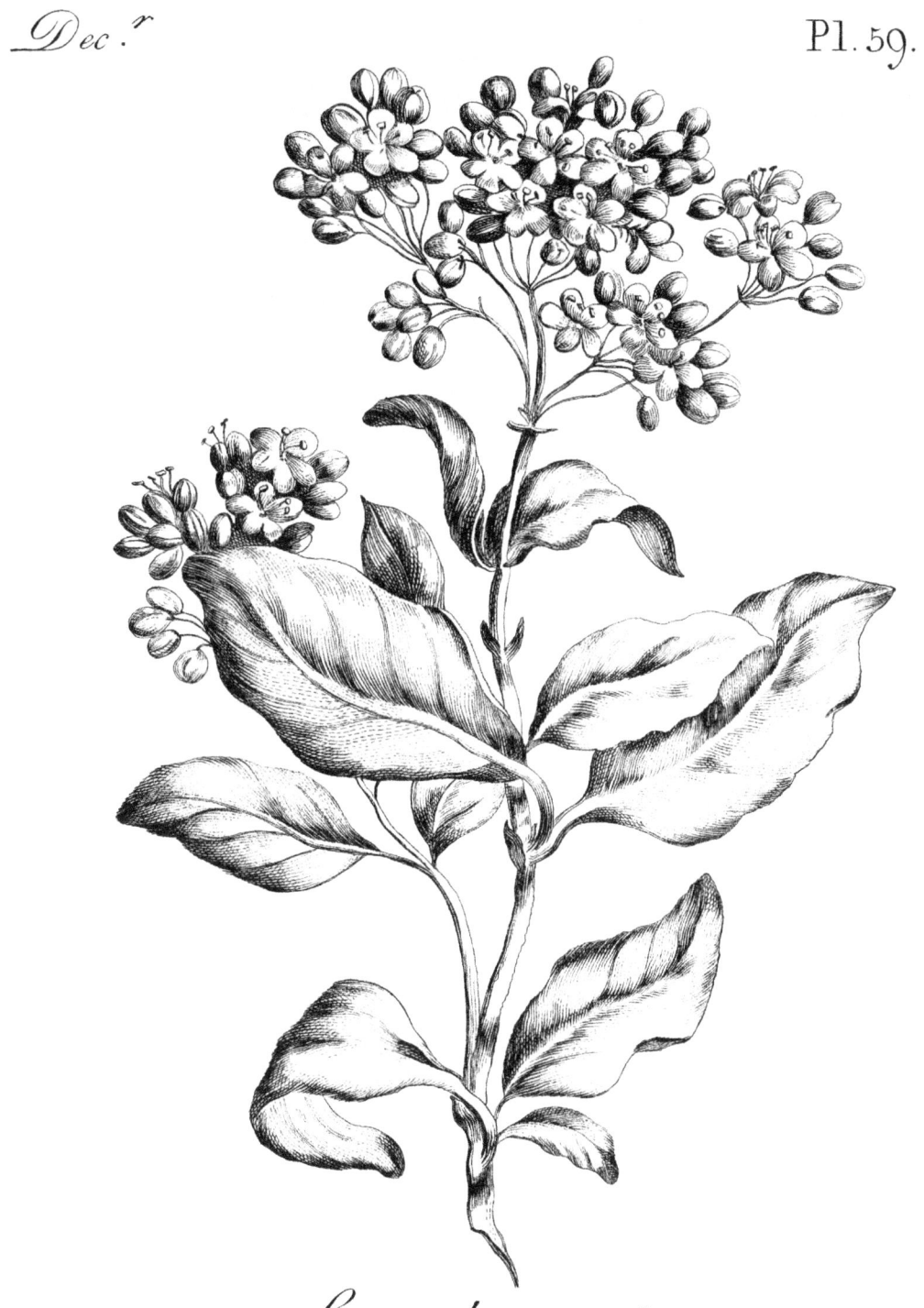

Laurelstina.

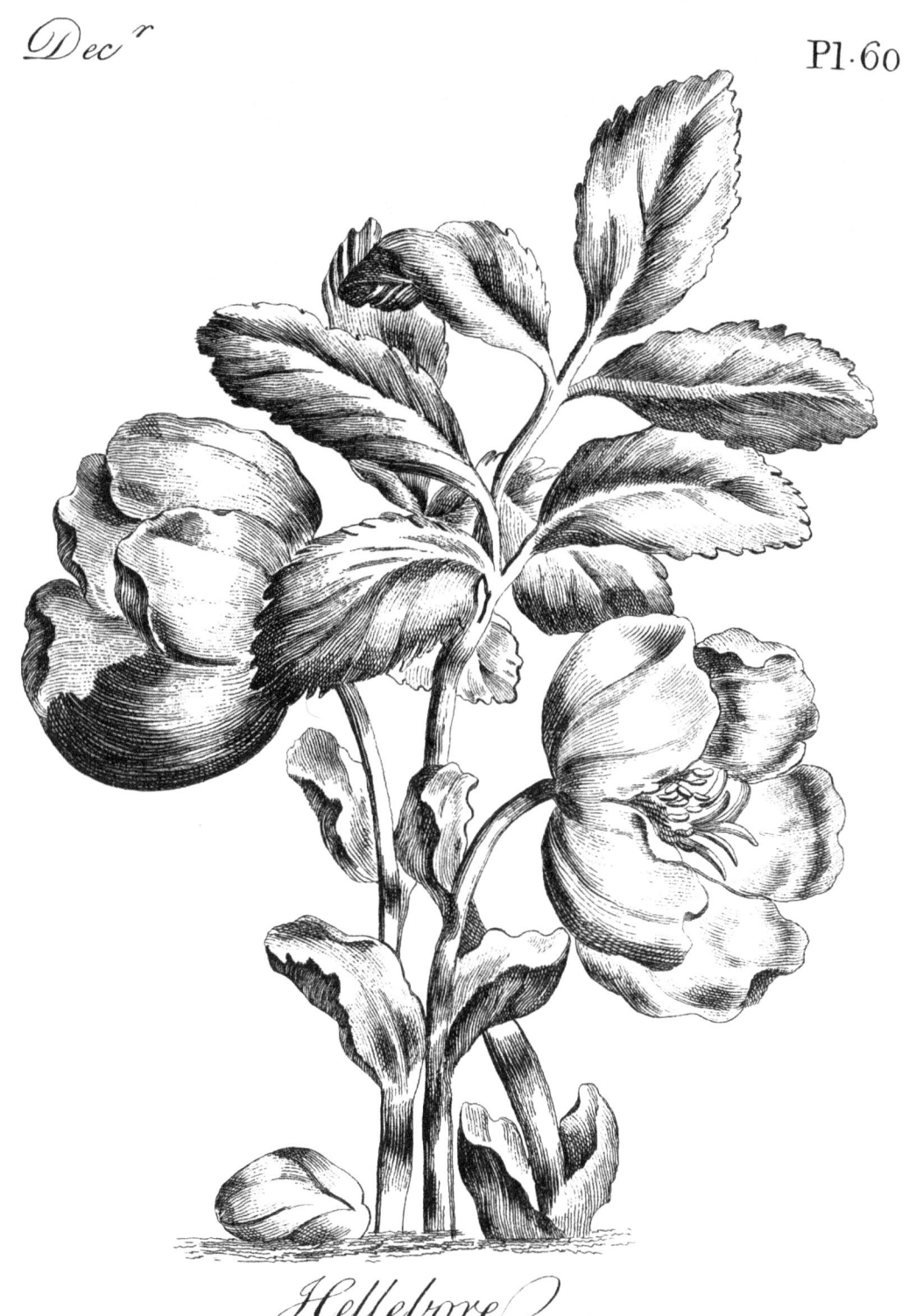

Hellebore.

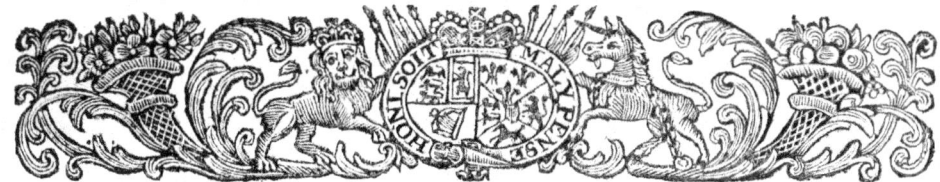

INTRODUCTION.

PAINTING having already had so many eloquent and powerful Advocates, it would now seem impertinent to tire the Reader in endeavouring to prove that Art noble and delightful. That it is so, the Ingenious have always, in the strongest Manner confess'd, by their constant Attention and Encouragement : Therefore, the only Use here made of an Introduction, will be to inform the Purchasers of this Work, of the Plan on which it is executed.

The Rules, which will be here laid down, for the executing the pleasing Branch of Painting, of which this Book is to treat, are the Result of real Practice, and deliver'd without the least Reserve. In Regard to the engrav'd Designs, it may be thought, that they might have been better represented by Copies from the great Masters, who have excell'd in Flower-Painting; such as *Baptiste, Vanhuyfom, Verelst*, &c. The Author is conscious of the Force of this Objection ; but as many prefer an original Work, for the sake of its original Particularity, it is here chose to draw them immediately from Nature.

Drawing from Flowers need not be loaded with mathematical Rules, yet there is one which we must always retain, in order to draw properly from Nature ; and that is, Flowers are suppos'd in general to be round when seen in Front, and to appear oval in Proportion, as they are more or less turn'd from the Eye : But a Circumstance of the greatest Consequence to an elegant Representation of this Part of Nature, is chusing the Flower in its proper State for Copying. The Gardener may admire his Flower when most regular and compact, but the most successful Painters have always chose to represent their Blossoms as ripen'd to a Degree of Looseness, subject to be folded and play in the Wind. By taking the Liberty here recommended, the Propriety of strict Drawing will still be adher'd to ; and the young Practitioner will happily avoid the lifeless Formality of flat Drawing, and the Errors of an unlimited Floridness. There are indeed many curious Plants that their own particular Beauties would appear formal in Painting, and they are therefore omitted, or only occasionally drawn, for the Use of the Botanist, when such Accuracy is requir'd, that the strictest Formality of Drawing cannot then become a Fault.

A   C O-

COLOURING

IS not here to be underſtood, as only the putting in the Colours preſented by Nature on the Flowers ; but likewiſe the Shadowing thoſe Colours, in ſuch a Manner, as to have the ſame Effect in the inner Parts of the Flower, as the Out-Line has to the Extremities. It is a general Rule in Painting, that the Light ſhould come in from the Left-Hand ; and, conſequently, the Right-Side of the Object muſt appear darkeſt ; But the Thinneſs of the *Petals**, in ſome Flowers, admitting the Light through them, there will happen neceſſary Lights to be ſhewn, tho' on the Right-Hand Part of the Flower ; which, in a more ſolid Subſtance, would appear abſolutely dark.

The Limits of the Work, and as I preſume, the Student's Deſire to come to the practical Part, occaſions the being as brief as poſſible on the Theory of the Study. The Painter, who may perhaps ſmile at the Plainneſs and intended Simplicity of theſe Inſtructions, ſhould conſider that this is a Work not addreſs'd to thoſe who are already Artiſts, but an Invitation to the young uninſtructed Admirers of Painting to the Practice of this delightful Branch of it.

The principal COLOURS *uſed in* FLOWER-PAINTING.

White, ———	Flake-White.
Reds, ———	Carmine, Lake, Vermillion, Red Lead.
Blues, ———	Ultramarine, Bice, *Pruſſian* Blue, Indico.
Green, ——	Sap-Green.
Yellows, ——	Gamboge, *French* Berries.
Browns, —	Gall-Stone,
Black, ———	*Indian* Ink.

Carmine

* *Petal* is the Term uſed in Botany to expreſs that Part, or Parts, of the Plant, which compoſe the Bloſſom. 'Tis neceſſary to make uſe of this one Term of that Science, as there will be Occaſion, in the Courſe of this Work, to deſcribe the particular Parts of the Flowers.

63

Carmine is to be temper'd in your Shell with Gum-Water ; and adding a little Spirits of Hartſhorn, when uſed for the pale Colour, it gives it a very pleaſant Bloom for Flowers.

Sap-Green, Gamboge, and *Indian* Ink, are only to be diluted with fair Water.

The Colour is to be extracted from the *French* Berries, by breaking them a little and pouring boiling Water on them, adding a little Allum.

The other Colours muſt be ground fine on a Stone, with Gum-Water proportion'd to their Quality.

Lake, *Pruſſian* Blue and Indico, being liable to crack, a little Sugar-Candy, diſſolv'd in weak Gum-Water, is preventive to that Inconveniency.

Gum-Arabic is what is uſed : 'Tis neceſſary to chuſe the cleareſt it being very eſſential to the Beauty of the Colours.

The Pencils are thoſe of Camels Hair. The youngeſt Practitioner need hardly be inform'd, that it is beſt to chuſe thoſe that taper to one and a fine Point, without being ſubject to ſplit at the Ends. For painting Flowers, they are beſt of a moderate Length in the Hair.

If the Colours ſhould happen not to work freely, occaſion'd by any Greaſineſs of the Paper, a little of the Gall of an Ox or a Fiſh, the latter being preferable, will greatly aſſiſt the Freedom of the Pencil.

N. B. Ladies and Gentlemen may be ſupply'd with the aforemention'd Colours, and all others, carefully prepar'd : Alſo all Materials for Drawing and Painting, at the moſt reaſonable Rates, by the Publiſher of this Work.

A 2   I N-

64

INSTRUCTIONS
FOR
COLOURING.

1. HYACINTH.

HYACINTHS are Blue, or White ; others are White, with a faint Tinge of Crimſon. The Blue Ones are began with Bice, ſhadowing, with *Pruſſian* Blue, and finiſhing with Indico. The light Parts may be work'd at Diſcretion, either leaving the Paper, by neatly ſhading with Bice, or by laying it all over and heightning with White. The White *Hyacinths* may be colour'd in the ſame Manner as the White *Lilly*. For thoſe with a Bluſh of Crimſon, a faint Tinge of Carmine muſt be tenderly waſh'd over, and finiſhing as directed for the White Ones. If Ultramarine is uſed inſtead of the Bice, it will make the Work appear more delicate. The Stalk and Leaves are a bluiſh Green, done with the ſame Mixture as the *Lilly*.

2. CYCLAMEN.

THIS Flower is a purpliſh Red. Its Stalk is Rediſh at the Bottom, and Whitiſh upwards. The Leaves are a deep Green on the Upper-Side, and a rediſh Purple underneath.

3. DOUBLE CROWFOOT.

THE Flower is Yellow ; the Stalks a whitiſh Green, ting'd with Red towards the Bottom ; the Leaves alſo a very pale Green.

HEN

65

4. HEN and CHICKEN DAISEY.

THE principal Flower is variegated with White and Red ; the Little Ones, which furround it, nearly all White ; the Stalks a pale Green, ting'd with Red at the Bottom ; the Leaves a pleafant Green.

5. COLCHICUM.

A Pale purplifh Crimfon is the Ground Colour of this Flower, which is fpotted with a deep Red ; the Leaves a deep Green.

6. CROCUS.

THE *Crocus* is either Yellow, very tenderly ftripp'd with Purple in the Middle of each *Petal* ; or pale Purple, ftripp'd with a deeper Tinct of the fame Colour : For the Colouring of which we refer the Practitioner to the Flowers of the fame Colour elfewhere treated of. The Leaves are a dark Green, with a White Vein up the Middle of each. The Film, which furrounds them at the Bottom, is a pale whitifh Brown.

7. SNOW-DROP.

THE Whole of this Flower is White, excepting an Edge of Green on the inner *Petals.* The Stalk is Pale, and the Leaves a bluifh Green.

8. DOUBLE HYPATICA.

THE Flower is a deep Blue ; the Stalk pale Green, ting'd with Red ; the Leaves deep Green.

9. DOUBLE VIOLET.

THE Flower is a deep Blue, with a Tinge of Purple ; the Stalks are a pale Green, ting'd with a redifh Purple towards the Bottom ; the Leaves a ftrong Green.

10. PASQUE FLOWER.

THE Flower is a rich bluifh Purple : the Stalk a whitifh Green, but Purplifh at the Bafe : the Leaves a pale whitifh Green ; their Foot-Stalks Redifh.

SINGLE

66

11. Single ANEMONE.

SOME *Anemone's* are Purple, others Scarlet, and others are pale ſtraw Colour, ſtripp'd or ſpotted with Crimſon. The Purple Ones are to be painted with a Mixture of *Pruſſian* Blue and Carmine, finiſhing the ſtrongeſt Parts with Indico. The Scarlet Ones are to be done according to the Directions given for the Scarlet *Martagon*, in *Page* 71. The Variegated Ones are to be firſt cover'd with a thin Waſh of Gamboge, ſhading with Biſtre. For the Crimſon Stripes or Spots, a Lay of Carmine, ſhading with the ſame Colour; for the dark Parts Indico. The Leaves may be done as thoſe of the *Guelder Roſe*. The Stalk is Brown.

12. MEZERION.

A Pale Crimſon is the Colour of the Flower when ſeen open; the Outſide much deeper; the Stem is Brown; the Leaves, which but juſt appear while the Flowers are in Bloom, are a pleaſant Green.

13. Double DAFFODIL.

THE Large Outer *Petals* are a pale Yellow; the Inner Ones deeper; and the Small Ones, partly underneath the Large Ones, Orange Colour. The Stalk and Leaves are to be done as the *Jonquil*, in *Page* 68.

14. Double ALMOND BLOSSOM.

THE Flower is ſomewhat deeper then the Single One; the other Parts are to be colour'd exactly the ſame.

15. ALMOND BLOSSOM.

THIS early and beautiful Flower is a pale Roſe Colour, ſomewhat inclining to the Purple. A very faint Waſh of Carmine muſt be laid all over, ſhadowing neatly with a reddiſh Purple, made with Carmine and a very little *Pruſſian* Blue. The Stem is Brown, done with Biſtre, finiſhing with Black. The Buttons are a pale Yellow. The Foot-ſtalks and Cups of the Flowers are a pale Green. Scarce any Leaves appear while the Flower is in Bloom, excepting a few beginning to ſhoot at the Ends of the Branches, which are a pleaſant Green; begun with Sap-Green, finiſhing with *French* Berries and Indico.

CROWN

67

16. CROWN IMPERIAL.

THIS Flower is a rich Orange-Colour; began with a Lay of Gamboge, and on that another of Red-Lead, fhadowing with Carmine. The Leaves, whch in a very fingular Manner crown the Flower, are to be done as directed for the Leaves of the *Guelder Rofe,* in *Page* 68. The Stalk is ting'd with Brown.

17. AURICULA.

THIS beautiful Flower is, by the Gardener's Art fo varied, that a particular Defcription of its Varieties would be endlefs. A much efteem'd Sort is to be colour'd thus: Begin with a pale Lay of Gamboge, fhadowing it with Biftre, leaving a broad Space round the Centre White; which Part is to be fhadow'd with *Indian* Ink, mix'd with Sap-Green: Then that Part which is begun with Gamboge is to be variegated with a purplifh Red, made by a Mixture of Carmine and *Pruffian* Blue. The Hollow in the Centre muft be a ftrong Yellow, fhadow'd with Gall-Stone. This done, it is to be neatly dotted with White, moftly on the Centre; mixing *Indian* Ink proportionably with the White, as the Flower becomes dark. The Stalk and Leaves are a greyifh Green, to be painted with a Mixture of of Sap-Green, White, and Indico; adding more Indico, for the Shades.

18. DAFFODIL.

THIS Flower, with its Stalk and Leaves, are be painted in the fame Mander as the *Jonquil,* defcrib'd in *Page* 68.

19. FRITILLARY.

A DULL redifh Purple is for the Ground Colour of this Flower, and check'd with a deeper Colour, or fometimes with a dufky Yellow. The Stalks and Leaves are a blue Green.

20. DOUBLE HYACINTH.

THIS Flower, with its Stalk and Leaves, are to be colour'd in the fame Manner as the Single One, defcrib'd in *Page* 64.

21. ANEMONE.

OF thefe Flowers, efpecially the Double Ones, there is fuch a Variety, and the Colours on them fo diverfify'd, that we can only mention the richeft Sorts, and leave the Practitioner to the Study of Nature, that inexhauftible Fund of Improvement. The large *Petals* are White, ftriped or clouded with

with Carmine. The fmall *Petals* are done with a pale Straw Colour, fhaded with neat Lines of Carmine, or Green made with Indico and *French* Berries, according to Fancy. The Stalk is Brown, by a Mixture of Carmine and Sap-Green, fhaded with Indico and Carmine. The Leaves Sap-Green, and finifh'd with *French* Berries and Indico.

22. PARROT TULIP.

THIS Flower differs in Shape greatly from the other Tulips, being jagg'd at the Edges ; and, from the Back of each Petal, appear Parts much refembling the Beak of a Bird ; from whence its Name.

23. GUELDER ROSE.

THIS Flower it White ; to be painted in the fame Manner as the White *Lilly*, making the dark Side pretty ftrong, in order to give Roundnefs to the Clufter. The Leaves are to be done with Sap-Green, fhading with Indico and French Berries. The Stem is a blackifh Brown, being woody ; to be done with Biftre, fhadowing with *Indian* Ink.

24. JONQUIL, DOUBLE *and* SINGLE.

BOTH thefe Flowers are a fine Yellow ; the Cup in the Middle of the Single One Orange-Colour, laid firft with Red-Led, over which a Lay of Gamboge, and fhadow'd with Carmine ; the darkeft Parts with Carmine and Indico. The other Parts of the Flower Gamboge, fhadow'd with Gall-Stone ; and, in the darkeft Parts, with Biftre and a little Carmine. The Stalks and Leaves are a bluifh Green, made with *Pruffian* Blue and Sap-Green ; adding Indico, in the darkeft Parts.

25. TULIP.

THIS Flower is not at all inferior to the *Carnation*, as to Variety, though fomewhat different in Difpofition of Colour, the *Tulip* being generally ornamented with Stripes of various Colours. Crimfons and Purples, upon either a White, Yellow, or Straw-Colour Ground, are the moft common. For the Mixtures and Shading which Colours, any Student, by recollecting the preceeding Direction, will be enabled properly to colour this Flower. The Leaves and Stalk may be done in the fame Manner of thofe of the *Carnation*.

26. ROSE.

THE Rofe is, and very juftly, the Favourite of the Painters ; feldom left out in any Compofition, where it can be admitted. Efteem'd for its natural Tendernefs of Colour, and Boldnefs of Shape, it furnifhes Matter for
the

the moſt maſterly Pencil. Our common Method of Colouring this Flower, is to begin with a Lay of thin Carmine; and to Shadow it, by uſing the Carmine in Degrees thicker, and conſequently darker. This Manner, by its gay Appearence at firſt, courts the Eye, but is evidently erroneous ; for notwithſtanding the fineſt Colours we can uſe are but Dirt, when compar'd with the natural Gaiety of the Tints on Flowers, yet the Colouring the Roſe with Carmine only, gives it a diſagreeable and unnatural Glare : To prevent which it is here recommended, after the firſt or lighteſt Carmine is laid on, to ſoften it with a faint Waſh of *Pruſſian* Blue, then proceed with pure Carmine ; and, to give Power to the darkeſt Parts of the Flower and Roundneſs to its Appearance, add a little Indico. If one is repreſented ſo much blown as to ſhew the Buttons in the Middle, they are firſt to be laid with Gamboge and ſhadow'd with Gall-Stone. The Stalks are browniſh, done with Sap-Green and a little Carmine ; adding Indico for the Shades, on the dark Side. The Upper-Sides of the Leaves are done with Sap-Green, ſhadow'd with *French* Berries and Indico mix'd together, to make a dark Green. The Barks, or Under-Sides, are a dulliſh Green, made with White, Indico and a little Sap-Green. It it not pleaſing in Nature, but to make ſome of the Leaves a yellowiſh Brown, as if withering, gives a natural and pleaſant Air in Painting ; which is to be done with a Mixture of Gamboge, Sap-Green, and Carmine.

27. R A N U N C U L A.

RANUNCULA's are variouſly colour'd : Some are White, edg'd or clouded with Crimſon ; others Straw-Colour, or Yellow, ſtriped with Scarlet, which may be executed acccording to the Directions given for other Flowers of the ſame Colour, a Repetition of the Mixture of the Colours being needleſs. The Leaves are done with Sap-Green, ſhadowing with Indico and *French* Berries ; taking the Liberty of making ſome Leaves Yellowiſh or Brown, which makes a pleaſing Variety in the Work. The Stalk is to be made Brown, by a Mixture of Carmine and Sap-Green.

28. I R I S.

THERE is a very great, if not unlimited, Variety in the Colouring of this Flower. The moſt common are Blue, with a Yellow Vein on each *Petal* ; others Pale Fleſh Colour, variegated with Purple or Blue, &c. The Colour of the Flower here repreſented, is as follows : The three upright *Petals* are White, to be painted according to the Directions for the *Narciſſus*, tinging the Baſs of each *Petal* with Gamboge. The other three *Petals* are Purple, with a Vein of Yellow ; beginning at the Baſe, and ending about the Middle. The Purple is done with a Mixture of Carmine and *Pruſſian* Blue ; beginning pale, and ſtriping it from the Centre with a deeper Colour, in the ſame Manner as repreſented in the Engravings, adding Indico for the ſtrongeſt Shades. The Leaves and Stalk are a bluiſh Green, done with Sap-Green and *Pruſſian* Blue, ſhadowing with the ſame Colour.

B   PIONY.

70

29. PIONY.

THIS Flower is a deep Crimſon ; begun with a ſtrong Lay of Carmine, proceeding with the ſame Colour, adding Indico proportionally, as the Shades grow darker. The Stalk is a pale Green, faintly ting'd with Brown, by waſhing ſlightly over the Sap-Green with Carmine. The upper Sides of the Leaves are a ſtrong Green, to be done with deep Sap-Green, ſhading with the Mixture of *French* Berries and Indico. The under Sides are paler.

30. DOUBLE WHITE NARCISSUS:

WHITE Flowers vary in their Shades, notwithſtanding their Ground Colour is alike. In ſome the dark Parts appear blueiſh, in others a little browniſh, others again have a greeniſh Tinge in the Shades. This Flower is to be done by leaving the Paper for the White, beginning the firſt or paleſt Shade with a Mixture of *Indian* Ink, Indico, and a very little Sap-Green, proceeding with the ſame Colour, uſing it thicker for the darkeſt Shades. The Bottom of each *Petal* is faintly tinged with Green ; and, in the Centre of the Flower, a ſmall Edge of Carmine ſurrounds a Tuft of ſmall *Petals*. The Stalk and Leaves are a blue Green, made with *Pruſſian* Blue and Sap-Green : ſhading with the ſame Colour, and deepen'd with Indico. The Scabbard, at the Bottom of the Flower, is a pale Brown, colour'd with Biſtre and Yellow mixed together.

31. CARNATION.

THERE is ſuch an infinite Variety of *Carnations*, that a particular Deſcription of them would be endleſs, being compos'd of the following Colours ; White, Crimſon, Scarlet and Purple ; and thoſe Colours ſo diverſified, that the Student may take the Liberty of his Fancy, without the Danger of deviating from what may happen in Nature. The Cup, Leaves and Stalk are a pale bluiſh Green, to be done with a Mixture of *Pruſſian* Blue, Sap-green and White, adding Indico for the darkeſt Parts.

32. GERANIUM.

THIS Flower is to be colour'd in the ſame Manner as the *Almond Bloſſom*, deſcrib'd in Page 66, only ſomewhat deeper. The Leaves are a pleaſant Green, with an Edge of pale Straw Colour, as repreſented in the Engraving. The Stalk is Green, tinged with Brown towards the Bottom.

MAR-

33. MARTAGON.

MARTAGONS, are some Yellow; others, a most rich Scarlet. The Yellow Ones are done with a pale Gamboge, shading with Bistre, Carmine and Yellow mix'd together, so as to make a pleasant Brown. At the Base of each *Petal* are neat Spots of strong Indico. The Stalks and Leaves are a pleasant Green; to be done with Sap-Green, and a very little *Prussian* Blue. The Bottom of each Leaf swells into a roundish Knob, which is considerably paler than the other Parts. The Scarlet Ones are to be smoothly laid with Red-Lead, shading with Carmine; adding Indico for the deepest Shades. The Style, Filaments and Buttons are Orange Colour; laid first with Gamboge, and shadow'd with Carmine.

34. POPPY.

THE Instructions given for the *Carnation*, in *Page* 70, are all that are requisite for this Flower; only observing that it is diversify'd by different Colours on the Edges of the *Petals*, not stripp'd or clouded as that Flower.

35. GLADIOLUS.

THIS Flower is Crimson, inclining to the Purple; begun with a strong Lay of Carmine, and neatly shading with a Mixture of Carmine and *Prussian* Blue. The Bottom of the Flower is White, shaded with a greenish Tinge, by a Mixture of *Indian* Ink and Sap-Green; neatly blending the Carmine with it, by fine Strokes of each Colour. The Leaves and Stalk, from the Beginning of the Flowers to the Top, are a Brown, made with Sap-Green and Carmine. The bottom Parts are a pleasant Green, with Sap-Green and a very little *Prussian* Blue; shading with the same Colour, and finishing with *French* Berries and Indico.

36. SUN-FLOWER.

THE *Petals* of this noble, though common Flower, are a fine Yellow, painted in the same Manner as the yellow Part of the *Jonquil*, described in *Page* 68. The Centre is a strong reddish Brown, made with Yellow, Carmine and Indico; using more Carmine and Indico for the deepest Shades. The Leaves and Stalk are a pleasant Green; done with Sap-Green, shadow'd with the same Colour, and deepen'd with Indico and *French* Berries.

37. LILLY.

LILLIES are either White, or Orange Colour. The White Ones are done by leaving the Paper for the lightest Parts; and shadowing with a Mixture of *Indan* Ink, Indico, and a very little Sap-Green; keeping (as has been

before

before recommended for the other Flowers) a proper Gradation of the Shades. The Buttons are Orange Colour, and the Style a pale Green. The Leaves and Stalk are a bluish Green, with a Mixture of Sap-Green and *Pruffian* Blue, finishing with Indico. The Orange-colour'd Ones are done in the fame Manner as the *Nafturtion*, in *Page* 74, fpotting the Infide of each *Petal* with Indico towards its Bafe. The Buds, while young, are Green, turning to the Orange as they ripen, which makes a pleafing Variety in the Colouring.

38. Double STOCK.

DOUBLE *Stocks* are a purplifh Crimfon, or variegated with White and Crimfon. The Clufter of fmall *Petals* in the Middle are green, which diffufes itfelf faintly on the larger Ones, and affords a pleafing Diverfity. The Stalk and Leaves are a whitifh Green.

39. AFRICAN.

AFRICANS are either Yellow or Orange Colour. The Yellow Ones are to be done according to the Directions in *Page* 68, for the Yellow Part of the *Jonquil*, either pale or deeper at Difcretion: And the Orange Colour Ones, as the *Crown Imperial*, *Page* 67. The Stalk and Leaves are a pleafant Green.

40. LARKSPUR.

LARKSPURS have all the Varieties of the *China After*. The Leaves and Stalk are a bluifh Green.

41. HOLYHOCK.

HHLYHOCKS vary, from the paleft Rofe Colours to the deepeft Crimfon. Some are White, which, in a Compofition, afford an agreeable Contraft to the other Flowers, by their beautiful Shape; but if reprefented fingly, 'tis eafily imagined, any of the other Colours are the moft interefting: For which the Method laid down in *Page* 68, for Painting the Rofe, will anfwer; ufing the fame Colours deeper, according to Fancy, preferving a proportionable Shade of Colour, that the deep Shades may not appear too fuddenly dark to drown the effect of the pale Colours. The Stalk and Leaves are a pale Green, to be done with Sap-Green mix'd with White, for the pale Colours; the fame Colour, only lefs White, for the next Shade, and adding a little Indico for the darkeft Shades.

PASSION

42. PASSION FLOWER.

THIS Flower is, in Nature, fo beautifully fingular in its Structure, that without the Advantage of Colour (in which it is alfo delightful) it would engage the Attention of every curious Obferver of Nature. The *Petals* are a greenifh White, to be painted with a Mixture of *Indian* Ink and Sap-Green, leaving the Paper in light Parts. The Threads are fo exactly fet and colour'd, as to form three Circles of different Colours, *viz.* The Outer-one Blue ; fhadow'd with *Pruffian* Blue. The next is White ; to be done by continuing the Stroke with Flake-White, making the Space between each Thread dark, with the *Indian* Ink and Indico. The Inner-Circle is a reddifh Purple ; done with a Mixture of Carmine, and a little *Pruffian* Blue. The Centre of the Flower is a pale Yellow. The five Buttons are Yellow in the Infide ; which is the Part moftly feen, by their curling back as foon as the Flower blows. The other Parts, which project from the Centre, are a pale Green, ; excepting the three Projections for the Top, which are Purple. The Bud is a pale Green, with a Tinge of Red at its End. The Leaves are a dark Green ; to be done with Indico, *French* Berries, and a little *Indian* Ink mixed together. The Stalk and Tendrils are made Brown, with Sap-Green and Carmine. The Religious have named this Flower, from a Suppofition of its Parts defcribing the Paffion of our Lord.

43. POMEGRANATE BLOSSOM.

THE Whole of this Flower, with its Cup, is a rich Scarlet ; to be begun with Red-Lead, and finifhing with Carmine. The Stalk and Leaves are a pleafant Green.

44. HONEY-SUCKLE.

THE Outfide of this Flower is begun with a Lay of Carmine mix'd with a little Lake, adding Indico for the dark Shades. Some Flowers, in the fame Clufter, are more purplifh than others ; which may be done at Difcretion, to make a Variety of Colour, by adding *Pruffian* Blue to the Carmine. The Infides of the *Petals*, which are fhewn by their fplitting and curling back at the Ends, are fome White ; others, Straw Colour. The White to be fhadow'd with *Indian* Ink, mix'd with a very little Sap-Green ; the Straw Colour with a very pale Lay of Gamboge, fhadow'd with Biftre. The Style and Buttons, feen at the Ends of the Flower, are a faint Green. The Stalks are a purplifh Brown, with Carmine and a little Sap-Green. The Leaves Sap-Green, fhadow'd with *French* Berries and Indico.

DOUBLE

45. Double CHINA ASTER.

THIS Flower varies in Colour from White, to the deepeft Crimfon, or blue Purple. The Centre in the Single Ones, is Yellow; the Stalk is Brown, and the Leaves a ftrong Green.

46. GUERNSEY LILLY.

THIS Flower is a beautiful pale Crimfon, and when feen in the Sunfhine, appears fpangled with Gold, beyond the Power of Art to imitate; fo that the Student muft be content with making it a delicate Crimfon, by Directions already given for Flowers of the fame Colour. The Leaves are a blue Green. The Stalk Green, ting'd with a redifh Brown towards the Bottom.

47. NASTURTIAN.

THIS Flower is, in Nature, the richeft Orange-Colour that can be conceiv'd. The beft Method of imitating is, by a Lay of ftrong Gamboge all over; upon that another of Red-Lead, leaving the Yellow in the lighteft Parts, and fhadowing very neatly with Carmine. On the two largeft *Petals*, feven or eight Lines muft be very correctly drawn, with a deep Purple, made with Indico and Carmine. The Stalks and Leaves are a pleafant Green, made with *Pruffian* Blue and Sap-Green, fhadow'd with the fame Colours.

48. HEART's-EASE.

THE two upper *Petals* of this Flower are a rich Purple: The other three Yellow, or Straw Colour, edg'd and otherwife ftain'd with Purple, or Olive Colour, with very fine Lines of a deep Purple; beginning at the Bafe, and fpreading delicately over each *Petal*. The Stalk and Leaves are a pleafant Green.

49. CONVOLVULUS.

BLUE is the principal Colour of the *Convolvulus*; but the Bafe is ftain'd with Yellow, which gradually becomes White, and fpreads itfelf in Rays like a Star in the Centre. The Leaves and Stalk are a whitifh Green.

50. ALTHÆA FRUTEX.

THE Flower is White, ftained with a redifh Purple at its Bafe. The Clufter of Buttons is Yellow. The Stalk dark Brown. The Leaves a pleafant Green.

FRENCH

75

51. FRENCH MARYGOLD.

THIS Flower is Yellow, ftripp'd with a deep Red: Sometimes the Whole is Red, and only ting'd with Yellow. The Stalk is ting'd with Brown. The Leaves a pale dullifh Green.

52. PERSICARIA.

THE Flower, while in Bud, is a deep Crimfon ; when open fo as to fhew the Infide of the *Petals*, is a very pale Colour. The Stem is Brown, and the Leaves a pleafant Green.

53. LYCHNIDEA.

THE Flower are a very pale Red, a little inclining to Purple. The Stalk is Green, ftain'd with a redifh Brown. The Leaves a pleafant Green.

54. DOUBLE NASTURTIAN.

THE Directions for Colouring the Single One in *Page* 74, will fully an-fwer for this Flower ; only obferving that the Lines on the two large *Petals* in that, are obliterated in this Double One.

55 ST. JOHN's WORT.

THE Whole of the Flower is a fine Yellow. The Stalk is ting'd with a purplifh Red. The Leaves are a bluifh Green.

56. POLIANTHOS:

THIS beautiful Flower, little inferior to the *Auricula*, is greatly vary'd in its Colour. The principal Colour is a pale or deep Crimfon ; likewife Purple in its feveral Degrees of Colour, edg'd generally with White or Yellow. The Centre or tubular Part, is Yellow. The Crimfon is firft laid with a pale Carmine, finifhing with Indico and Carmine. The Yellow with Gamboge, fhadowing with Gall-Stone; and the darkeft Parts with Biftre. The white Edge muft be neatly drawn with Flake White ; if Yellow, to be wafh'd with pale Gamboge upon the White ; obferving where the Flower is in the Shade, to mix a little Biftre with the White for its Edge. The upper Sides of the Leaves are a pleafant Green ; to be colour'd with Sap-Green, and finifhing with a Mixture of Yellow Berries and Indico, making them appear rough, by fudden Dafhes of a deep Colour, as exprefs'd in the Print. The under Sides are a dull whitifh Green; to be done with the Colours defcribed in *Page* 68, for the *Rofe* Leaves. The Stalk is brown, with a Mixture of Sap-Green and Carmine.

WALL

76

57. WALL-FLOWER.

THE Common Ones are Yellow ; a richer Sort, call'd The *Bloody Wall*, Yellow, ftain'd with Crimfon very deep on the Under-Side of the *Petals*, and faintly vein'd on the upper. The Cup of the Flower is a purplifh Brown. The Stalk and Leaves a bluifh Green.

58. ACONITE.

THE Flower is Yellow, furrounded by Leaves of a ftrong Green. The Stalk is Whitifh, ting'd with Brown near the Flower.

59. LAURELSTINA.

THE Flower, when open, is White ; but while in Bud, only fhewing the Under-fide of the *Petals*, is a redifh Brown. The Stalk is alfo a redifh Brown. The Leaves a pleafant Green.

60. HELLEBORE, or CHRISTMAS ROSE.

THE Flower is White, ftain'd at the Bafe of each Petal with Crimfon. The Buttons a pale Yellow. The Stalk is a pale Green, fpotted with Crimfon. The Leaves a ftrong Green.

FINIS.